Date Due

MUSIC

A Living Power in Education

A COMPENDIUM OF THE WRITINGS

OF **RUSSELL VAN DYKE MORGAN**

EDITED BY HAZEL NOHAVEC MORGAN

SILVER BURDETT COMPANY

New York   Chicago   Dallas   San Francisco

PREFACE

In every area of education certain individuals can be identified whose thinking and devotion to ideals have had a marked and lasting influence. Such a person was Russell VanDyke Morgan, whose activities during the past three decades have made a permanent imprint upon the program of music education in the schools of America.

Dr. Morgan was a planner for the future. He always took leadership in testing the new and putting into practice all that proved to be valuable. His mind was busy with ideas based upon a vision of future developments in music education. This compendium of his writings will not only preserve his thinking but will serve as a guide for those whose torches have been lighted by his dynamic influence.

The material contained in this book has been assembled from manuscripts of lectures, articles, bulletins, and teaching notes which, for the most part, have not been published previously. No effort has been made to cover all phases of music education, but rather to assemble and present the available material under selected natural headings. Except where adjustments were necessary for the sake of continuity, the exact wording of the author has been maintained.

HAZEL NOHAVEC MORGAN
Northwestern University, 1953

iii

"Because he has shared so generously his accurate understanding and profound appreciation of the finest in music;

"Because young minds catching sparks from the flame of his genius have developed a cultural background leading to better citizenship;

"Because those touched by the magic spell of his personality have come to understand the spiritual values of music, and through his teachings have been made stronger in character and have been inspired with nobler ideals, this book has been edited and published."

Quoted with the exception of the last seven words from the presentation speech made by Dr. Morgan on the occasion of Dr. Walter Damrosch's receiving the American Educational Award of the Associated Exhibitors (1934).

CONTENTS

"I am quite overwhelmed with the feeling that I should have something of supreme importance to contribute to my profession.

"However, I have resolved to put aside hope for this great inspiration and to just plod along with my own normal thinking, letting my ideals color everything I say or do."

R.V.M.

BASIC PHILOSOPHY

FOR MUSIC EDUCATION

*"The many fields of knowledge that we have
are but windows through which the human soul
can look out upon a significant and beautiful
universe. As fine as music is, it is only one window, and a good life calls for a broader vista
than one single direction. I claim that music
always has been a highly significant emotional
and aesthetic stimulus in human life and that
to weave it into the fabric of American life will
do much to create a thrilling and hopeful dawn
for humanity in this new world."*

R.V.M.

Whenever some cataclysmic event occurs in world
history, humanity instinctively thinks of it as an opportunity
to change the purposes and practices of life. At times there
seems basis for hope that there will be a revolution in the
lives of people. History does not give us any foundation for
such a belief. On the contrary, most of the patterns of living
have been an evolution or gradual change in outlook, activity, and basic philosophy. There are in existence many great

1

principles having eternal truth which must not be forgotten but used as a foundation for ever-expanding development.

Music and a New World. It is evident that America has placed too much emphasis on its remarkable material achievement in the scientific field, with the projection of that human search for knowledge, until it has reached the present state of using atomic powers for better or for worse. The human spirit is presently appalled by the fact that advancement of knowledge is not necessarily for the good of humanity. It is my personal belief that we will realize more and more that it is the *will* and *purpose* of humanity that is the greatest concern of the present day, and that this should be the directing force for the enormous potential power at our command.

Perhaps today's condition is to be expected when we realize that the aim of education has been primarily concerned with only the intellectual phase and has been seemingly blind to the necessity of developing the spiritual, emotional, and aesthetic aspects of human life. If we, as music teachers, can help in bending the direction of our educational program toward greater emphasis upon these spheres of human growth, there is the possibility of developing a people who will wholeheartedly and effectively use all of our material resources and scientific knowledge for the good of humanity. César Franck, in a moment of true insight, made this statement: "Music is both a craft and an art." No one would deny the necessity for craftsmanship in music or any other of the avenues of activity about us, but it would be tragic if, in our concern for the development of technical proficiency, we do not develop a program for balancing that craftsmanship with the *spirit* of art.

Properly taught, music can provide a remarkable example of true democracy wherein both the individual and society have due regard for each other. The dignity and worth of the individual must always be protected, and yet it is necessary that the individual feel his responsibility to society as a whole. This is true democracy, the American way of life, and we in the music education field can do much to develop a true balance in this matter for our young people.

One thing greatly needed in America is a crusade urging students to use their talents for the betterment of the community in which they live. There is altogether too much thought of their being developed so that they may go to some far-off place and become famous. Perhaps it will be difficult to change this thinking so long as emphasis is placed more upon the performer than on the music to be performed. It is to be hoped that the day will come when people will be far more interested in knowing *what* opera, symphony, string quartet, or oratorio is to be performed than in *who* is the conductor or soloist.

We have made great strides in America. Consider the fact that we have some four hundred organized symphony orchestras with paid conductors and many thousands of choruses and choirs which show an increasing respect for good musical literature and good performance. Perhaps the need now is to broaden our activities to include more interest in such things as chamber music, home ensembles, and group music wherever it can operate to the betterment of human living.

It would be foolish to think of music as the only saving force in the world. The many fields of knowledge that we have are but windows through which the human soul can look out upon a significant and beautiful universe. As fine as music is, it would be only one window, and a good life calls for a broader vista than one single direction. I do claim that music always has been a highly significant emotional and aesthetic stimulus in human life, and that to weave it into the fabric of American life will do much to create a thrilling and hopeful dawn for humanity in this new world.

Many of us teachers have a positive genius for completely

separating our philosophies of music education and our actual practices in music education. Everyone will agree that our practice should be merely the expression of our philosophy, but all too often I have seen committees of teachers spend hours of hard and thoughtful work in preparing a philosophy as a foundation for a course of study. Then I have observed these same people reverently place that philosophy on a shelf and go on about the work-a-day business of teaching school, without bothering to develop procedures that will actually bring that philosophy to the children in the classroom. Both philosophy and the practice of implementing it are obvious needs.

Permanent Values. The contemporary period at any point in the history of the world has seemed to be chaotic and confusing to those who were living at that time. As we gain historical perspective, the confusion and uncertainty resolve into a clarified picture in which much of the activity disappears permanently and only a few important and significant items remain. There are deeply significant events occurring today, side by side with those chattering inconsistencies which seem to overpower us and blind us to the really good things.

There are some values which are permanent. These are the enrichments that come to human life through activity in and understanding of the fine arts.

First to be mentioned is the development of integrity and ideals within the individual. We all recognize the tremendous urge toward accomplishment and social responsibility that comes from well-directed experiences in music and the other arts.

Second, there is the development of an attitude that will place opportunity above security. One of the marks of energetic youth is the desire to seek out new and better ways rather than to be confined to a security that sooner or later becomes dull and commonplace to the one who chooses it.

Third, I believe that the aesthetic and emotional enjoyment of the fine arts will always have an important place in living, and that those who have equipped themselves with this power to understand and appreciate music, literature, and art have achieved one of the great fundamentals for a happy and successful life.

Fourth, a recognition that power and ability can come only through a slow, solid growth and that the exercise of patience in waiting for fruition is of utmost importance.

Every student who has taken hold of these fundamental ideas may feel that he has been equipped with the power to help himself in reaching an understanding of what this life is all about. Temporary adjustments are needful. Humanity turns from certain demands for artistic performance only to emphasize its desire for artistry in some new form of expression. Our real purpose is not to attempt to turn back to old forms of expression, but to discover new avenues and to adjust the eternal values of artistic effort into channels of activity that humanity demands at the present moment. The real challenge in all fields of fine arts today is to discover how best to bring satisfaction to our fellow beings through permanent aesthetic values, for from the very beginning this has been one of the greatest hungers of mankind.

Everyone is aware that we have been going through a striking period of renaissance in the field of music. There are many reasons for this. Perhaps the greatest of all is the prevalence today of radio and television and the many fine musical programs available through these media. We have heard and seen great singers, players, and orchestras. They have set up for us standards of taste and discrimination that have acted in a miraculous way toward bringing the finest expression in the arts to an interested and appreciative audience. Side by side with this great expansion of musical opportunity for the listener has been the development of a program of music education in our schools that will help make all citizens appreciate more richly and fully the beauty that is theirs for the asking.

A *Social Attitude toward Music Education.* One sometimes senses a line of battle drawn sharply between two opposing social concepts, one insisting that the worth of our educational process is measured by the products men are taught to produce and the other holding to the proposition that the purpose of education is to develop men possessing the power to live richly.

The social objective can cause real harm if it ignores the artistic qualities in performance. There are enthusiastic exponents of the social values who fail to realize that activity is not necessarily purposeful *per se.* These individuals, believing in the good of musical participation, seem not to see the necessity of guarding musical quality. While granting that it is proper for the social aim to come first, it can still be insisted that unless artistic values rise consistently, the whole activity will disintegrate and become worthless.

It is my personal conviction that the first purpose of music education is to enrich the lives of human beings, both as individuals and in groups. In order to carry out this intention, however, we need to use a constantly higher quality of musical literature and an improving skill and understanding, if interest is to be maintained and a permanent enrichment of personality assured. This is the true social attitude which music educators should maintain.

The social and artistic values must be reconciled and made to serve each other rather than remain in seeming conflict. Art values that do not enrich humanity are worthless, but it is just as clear that the social purpose of music cannot be realized unless artistic values serve as a guiding factor.

6

A strong development of social values can be secured through proper music instruction. The music class is a practical situation in which the individual contributes to the welfare of the group and the group activity increases the social and artistic equipment of the individual. Each boy and girl must participate to the fullest extent of his or her ability in order that the group result may be acceptable. The individual receives inspiration and good from the contributing activity of all his co-workers. As a member of a musical organization, he is conscious of the failure in the group result if any individual member does not contribute his best. In other words, the student learns that the good of the group depends upon his individual contribution and, at the same time, that his own good depends on every other member contributing his share.

A child may experience keen delight in contact with some musical beauty and, though that child may never again hear music, the expansion of soul caused by that brief glimpse into the infinite will remain throughout life. So let us feel confidence in teaching well done, though the individual may never continue the activity in adult life. However, a proper basic philosophy gives us hope that many will be impelled to draw continually closer to the source of beauty and live more richly than they otherwise would.

2 CURRICULUM

"The air is filled with an ever-increasing appreciation of values that exalt and do not destroy. This is the moment for educators to contribute richly, through music, to a renaissance of the powers within the individual."

R.V.M.

In all the schools of our nation, a serious, continuing study is being made of the curriculum. In general, three concepts or definitions of the term, curriculum, are used. They are, *first*, a catalog of the various subjects offered by a given school; *second*, an outline of materials and problems within the boundaries of a given subject; and *third*, a series of significant experiences, each valid in its own right, and each based upon the powers and understandings developed through preceding experiences.

We are concerned here only with the third interpretation. Whenever a subject has reached the point of having a curriculum which is set and inflexible, just then does the spirit and vitality of educational experience disappear, and in their place is found sterility and weakness. This statement is so easily illustrated in the musical field. Music is above all else a living, vibrating experience and the purpose of all instruction is pointed toward making this experience broader and

8

deeper. Yet in many instances the formalized instruction in techniques and skills, which has become paramount, defeats the real purpose of music education. In spite of the constant bombardment of books, papers, and clinics devoted to curriculum study, it seems worth while to discuss this matter further so that we can keep before us continually the fact that the primary purpose of the curriculum is to provide for significant experiences. All of the courses of study and outlines upon which we devote such careful thought are of value only as they contribute to the most efficient handling of whatever experiences touch the student.

The distinctive feature of music education in the public schools of America is that the programs must be conceived and carried out in a way that will benefit all the children of a community. This comprehensive point of view does not envision identical musical experience for all pupils, but rather sees the need for varied opportunity to provide differentiation for all levels of music ability, so that each student may advance at his best rate of speed consistent with thoroughness.

The world is a remarkable reservoir of aesthetic pleasures, but no human has responded perfectly or fully to all of them. The reason for this is that our approaches and concepts are twofold: (1) intensity of penetration into the field of one art, and (2) breadth in the matter of response to various fields. This statement should serve as a fundamental guide in developing a music program. Music experience and the instruction necessary to illumine and interpret that experience is the right of every child. However, some of our pupils do have abilities and interest in the field of music. This makes it necessary for us to include in the curriculum intensive courses in music education as well as courses which will satisfy a breadth of interest.

Curriculum Construction. To be effective, curriculum construction must make use of the following steps: *first,*

9

the development of a philosophy; *second*, establishment of objectives growing out of this philosophy; and *third*, formulation of procedures and techniques to carry out the program. Incidentally, it is imperative to set up means of measurement or evaluation in order to know that the process is complete and to what extent the goal has been attained.

One of the problems in music education has been to develop ourselves as teachers to such a high point in musical ability that we can clearly and fairly evaluate the musical experiences we are seeking for our students. It is extremely difficult to measure aesthetic values, but the procedure of testing factual material is simple to plan and execute. Probably for that reason we have continually based grades of students and judgment as to their musical accomplishment almost entirely on the factual material, rather than on what should be the primary objective as indicated in our philosophy—the growth of aesthetic power.

Set programs of courses and routines for these courses menace aesthetic values. If there could be some way of suddenly obliterating the accepted and set teaching routine in a school, it is my judgment that educational values would increase measurably, although it must be admitted that the weak teacher without sufficient background and imaginative power would be lost and have only chaos in the class. It has often seemed to me that rigid courses of study exist in inverse ratio to the power of the faculty.

Aspirations for an ideal music education curriculum do not submit easily to the rigid boundaries of reality. Success seems to rest upon a balance of two faculties: (1) the power to soar, imaginatively, in the field of philosophy, and (2) the power to face clear-eyed the restrictions which reality places about one. It is only as we interpret ideal situations in terms of possibilities in our own specific situation that we can make educational progress and set up a program of music study which will be satisfactory and advantageous to all.

Any well-constructed course of study is necessarily made by teachers, because in no other way are teachers prepared to carry out the course of study. They have not grown up to it if some one person, such as a supervisor, sits in a study and constructs a program all by himself. Of course, the first thing to be accomplished is to make everyone aware of the existence of an adequate music program in the school. It should be recognized that any sane person will want to know three things right away: (1) Just where are we now in our music program? (2) Where are we going? (3) How do we propose to get there? Then he will ask: Why do we need to go? Why go there at all? We must be able to answer these questions to the satisfaction of laymen, educational theorists, and administrators of school systems, or we will not be able to put into practice the program of studies in music which we know are good.

In the Elementary Schools

A survey of music education in the elementary school division indicates that it is possible to set up seven types of experiences for the general music course offered to children in these elementary grades. Briefly they are as follows:

1. A wide experience in rhythmic activity and organized control of rhythm patterns. This would include pulsation, accentuation, and figuration.
2. The singing of a great body of beautiful song material especially suited to children's needs. This would include folk songs, art songs, and songs written especially for children.
3. A program of listening to musical literature that is technically beyond the ability of children to perform but musically of value to them. This should include both vocal and instrumental literature.
4. Opportunity for exploration of musical instruments. This

11

will provide an avenue for basic music learning, as well as satisfying interest or curiosity, and will aid in the discovery of unusual talent. Instrumental instruction should be provided for these talented pupils.

5. Experiences in self-expression. This should extend from free rhythmic response to the writing of music.

6. An organized program of ear training intended to develop three abilities, simultaneously rather than successively:
    a. A keen sensitiveness to musical sounds.
    b. An intelligent comprehension of these musical sounds.
    c. The building up of retentive powers so that a succession of musical sounds may remain in the mind as a musical idea.

7. A program for the development of the eye directed towards music reading; that is, the power to understand and reproduce in sound the printed musical notation. This is in reality a dual program, that of reading readiness and the development of music reading skill.

In carrying out this curriculum for the elementary school division, there will be, of course, general music instruction for all children, supplemented by a variety of musical activity for those of stronger interest and talent. These additional activities could be special choirs, orchestra, band, instrumental classes, educational concerts, composers' clubs, operettas and cantatas, as well as various concerts and other public appearances.

In the Junior High School

A variety of items should be considered in preparing a music program for this age group. There is at this age a lessening of interest in the theoretical aspect of music and a decided growth of interpretive power. The children become restless and uninterested in a music lesson consisting largely of sight singing and theory, yet this very thing seems fascinating to a fourth grade. The interpretive power, while very delicate and easily crushed under inexpert handling, is without question the major consideration in the junior high school music program.

As a basis for this music program, there should be a required course for all three grades which usually comprise this level. This course must combine the elementary and senior high school types of music activity and provide for sight singing and theory work in groups no larger than thirty to forty. There must also be provision for choral singing with larger groups of from sixty to eighty. This plan, as can be readily seen, provides for more or less individual attention in the smaller class and also the wonderful community interest that can be aroused only through singing in larger groups.

The mechanical problems inherent in designing a required music course are many. First of all, there is the need for at least two separate outlines for this age; one for classes in which only unchanged voices are present, and the other for classes containing the bass or baritone voice. The situation in which segregation of boys and girls is practiced demands considerable experimentation. Suitable material is rather difficult to find for boys that are segregated, but plenty of good part material is available for girls.

The practice of assigning students to various groups through mental tests puts a severe strain on music programs. Shall we direct the bulk of our work towards the highest, lowest, or intermediate group? The students involved have varying abilities in music and this creates a problem which cannot be ignored. It seems to me that we must decide on fundamentals to be taught, build our course upon these, and provide additional material that will greatly enrich the work for the groups with higher intelligence quotients. This plan does not carry the bright child in a vertical motion, that is, to grades above; but permits growth in a horizontal fashion by providing for a greater acquaintance with the beauties of music upon the same plateau of difficulty.

Most of the music work offered at the junior high school level should be planned for students of average ability. The boys and girls with little or no interest in music are, after all, few in number and are found usually among those with low scores on mental tests. The required music course for this uninterested group should contain few technical problems and a maximum amount of simple rote material. A large portion of the time could well be given over to rhythmic activities, listening lessons, and the singing of easy folk songs. The voices within this group are more mature, so many bass voices may be found even in the seventh grade. The mentally slow are difficult to adjust in a program planned for the child of normal age. However, they should neither be ignored nor allowed to take an undue proportion of the teacher's time.

A wealth of special classes should be contained in the curriculum for the musically talented children. Glee clubs and choral clubs, bands and orchestras, harmony and appreciation classes can give wonderful enrichment to the musical child's life. These classes should be elective, of course, and meet often enough to provide for real accomplishment. Discouragement and failure follow in the path of classes meeting only once a week. Many of these classes can meet five days a week to advantage, but the real educational values depend almost entirely upon the training and personality of the teacher.

It is an established fact that the junior high school age is particularly adapted to rapid instrumental development. A year's intensive study at this age will bring more accomplishment than the spending of twice that time four or five years later. Instrumental classes will provide a means for discovering latent talent that can be of real value to society and to the individual. Ability discovered in this way is rarely denied opportunities for continuing a musical education, but the business of preparing professionals is not the only purpose of this work. The ability to play an instrument, even if only moderately well, provides the means to spend leisure time profitably, with others of like inclination. It leads to the development of that person most happy among men, the musical amateur.

In the Senior High School

Upon reaching the senior high school level of education our boys and girls are offered more intensive specialization and the central core of required subjects is not as extensive as in the grades below. This means that in the majority of secondary schools, young people have a choice of different subjects from which to construct their complete program. There is usually no required music courses for all students, but a series of music classes are available to those whose inclination and interest lead them to elect music as a part of their curriculum.

Here again the music courses offered fall into two general groups, applied music and theoretical music and history.

Every musician is aware of the musical power of our a cappella choirs, glee clubs, orchestras, and bands today. These activities, however, are all classified as applied music, and it is only in scattered large communities that any great progress has been made in introducing courses in music history and music theory. Again, these schools are serving today as beacon lights and there is at present a movement which seems to possess real strength looking toward the development of an adequate offering in the field of such music fundamentals as ear training, sight singing, harmony, etc. There is likewise a developing interest in offering music history, which promises to be of considerable significance.

15

These various activities have given rise, in some degree, to the problem that faces the school of formulating some requirements for a balanced program, for the boy or girl who studies music. It is probably acceptable to allow the casual student to participate freely in applied music, with a definite limitation however on the amount of credit he may receive. There is a large portion of high school students who will treat music as a casual activity, or interest; just as they may make a brief study of biology or history, not for the purpose of becoming scholarly in that field, but in order to possess some contact with the broad activity of mankind. But in the case of a student who wishes to major in music, there needs to be machinery set up to make sure of a balanced experience in the field of applied music, theory, and history, much as though it were on the basis of the laboratory and the theoretical classroom.

The next step in the development of the music program should be an elective course designed for the young people with a casual interest in music who, after all, have some legitimate curiosity about music and would like to be cultured enough, perhaps, to be intelligent about some of the greater composers and the master works, just as most of us really want to know something about outstanding writers and their literature, or about great artists and their works. I call this a "layman's course" and it calls for a new type of treatment in teaching and for a teacher not normally the product of present-day training courses. The demand for this new teacher may be slow to show itself, but universities and colleges should consider the problems incident to the training needed for that work.

What follows is a description of a type of music curriculum occasionally found in the secondary school which seems to me to possess real value.

Applied Music. The *first* large division of this high school curriculum is applied music. In the choral field it is possible to maintain three distinct levels of instruction. First would be mixed choruses for students of ordinary talent and power. Proven ability in such a group would advance them to either the girls' or boys' glee club, which would be considered the second level. From these two groups would be chosen the members for the a cappella choir, which can well be designated as the highest level.

The same type of organization would be possible in the field of instrumental music; namely, elementary classes and ensembles for beginners, the preparatory band and orchestra for intermediate students, and the symphony orchestra and concert band for students with the greatest ability. In connection with this course we need to have a rather extensive program of ensemble training in both vocal and instrumental fields.

Theoretical Music. The *second* large division of the secondary school music curriculum would be in the field of theoretical music. It is not so simple to secure agreement as to the best organization, but from experience in my own situation I have come to feel that the following organization of the curriculum would serve the purpose best.

In the tenth grade there would be a course in theoretical music, perhaps called "Fundamentals of Music," aimed at mastery of the elements of musical theory, and including a strong rhythmic program, ear training, and sight singing.

In the eleventh grade there would be a continuation of the program in a course which added a study of chord relations, under the name of harmony. That, perhaps, is as far as the theory program should go except in an occasional school with a high enrollment of young people intending to follow music as a vocation, where more advanced theory courses could be offered in the twelfth grade. Personally, I believe that this advanced course should be treated from the modern view, with emphasis upon musical materials.

The weakness in the music history courses hitherto offered in senior high schools has been largely one of prerequisites; that is, so many of the students entering such a course lack the needed musical experience to make the course of any real value. By including in the school curriculum the general layman's course in music mentioned previously, it would be possible to assign all students without musical background to the layman's course and those with rich musical training to the history course, thus giving a more valuable opportunity to each of the two groups.

The study of music with private teachers outside the school is fairly general. Students asking for credit for such work must be required to enter some music class within the school. In no other way can the teacher of music in the high school become acquainted with the pupil's development. The only sane basis for such credit is through quarterly or semester examination, by competent persons appointed by the school. These examinations ought to be based upon a carefully organized course of study provided by the school; but specific music materials should not be required, except perhaps for one or two numbers performed for each examination.

Music appreciation, as a high school course, has come to mean anything or nothing. No music course should be permitted in the school program unless it contributes directly to the appreciation of music. If a choral or instrumental class is well conducted, it is a constant course in appreciation. On the other hand, the amount of material and the type of material is somewhat limited in these two groups. It should be remembered that unorganized listening has small value and a dry study of facts in history is almost worse than useless. This accounts for the combination of history of music and music appreciation which is frequently found in school programs.

I have a deep conviction that the great step forward in

music education in America will be taken when the aesthetic, emotional, and spiritual life of the high school pupil gets the active attention which it deserves. It is possible that our secondary schools have concerned themselves too much with the material or tangible things of this life and with the techniques of living together in one world, but have overlooked the obligation of so equipping each individual that his life will be interesting and rewarding whether he is alone or with a group.

The sense of beauty about which Santayana [1] writes so movingly can truly become one of the riches which the world cannot take away. The "well-furnished mind" is a priceless possession, becoming more valuable with every year. It is true that we must equip young people to support themselves and to have needed knowledge of the world in which they live, but it is at least as important to teach them how to see, hear, and enjoy the beautiful experiences that are available to them in this good world.

Ultimately the secondary school will realize the need for another or different faculty member in addition to those now catalogued as vocal and instrumental teachers. This new music teacher will be well equipped with a knowledge of musical literature, musical history, and theory, as well as being a person whose obvious delight in music is contagious. When such provision for the welfare of students is made, then we can say truthfully that we are adequately providing music education for *all* of America's young people. It is not a question of doing less for those now in our music classes, but answering the need of the others who will become the great consuming public in a truly musical America.

[1] George Santayana, *The Sense of Beauty*. New York: Charles Scribner's Sons, 1896.

3 BASIC OBJECTIVES IN SECONDARY SCHOOL MUSIC

"Education is coming more and more to the belief that the value of our civilization is not measured by things that man can be taught to produce, but by the manner of man produced."

R.V.M.

I have been unusually interested in making as thoughtful a study as possible of what some of the aims in school music should be. It is very easy for the instructor to say, "Why, yes, I know what I am trying to do," but when asked why he believes in some particular thing and how he regards its importance in comparison with other objectives, he is apt to become more and more uncertain as to just exactly what he is trying to do.

In the first place, the usual answer to the above question is, "I am trying to perfect an organization that can play or sing good music well." That is in itself a fine thing to do, but why do it? In other words, is the objective the production of beautiful music, using our young people as so much raw material in the process, or is the real answer that such an activity will bring richer appreciation into the lives of the

20

participants? It should be definitely established that our music program, vocal and instrumental, is set up primarily for the student and only incidentally for the music. This is the fundamental difference between professional and school music organizations.

Let us assume that we agree that our American school music program is primarily for the children; it then becomes our problem to decide what are the phases of this program and what contributions each makes toward the whole. With that purpose in mind, I am setting up three general objectives: (1) aesthetic, (2) social, and (3) technical.

By the aesthetic values of music I mean the power it has to arouse in the breasts of the performer and auditor alike an exaltation of spirit, a fine and ennobling feeling that to me represents the God-like in man. The social power of music is of scarcely less importance. This refers to the development of a will on the part of an individual to so use his talents in a group that the result will be a perfect bit of cooperative effort. In itself, technique is of secondary value, but because it is essential in securing the first two objectives, it becomes of major importance.

Aesthetic Objectives. Let us consider how the aesthetic values may be emphasized in our secondary school music program. We are apt to forget that music is a language and has something to say which cannot be given to the world through any other medium of expression. The use of the word "language" is perhaps a bit unfortunate. It seems to imply that music is merely another method of expressing the incidents of everyday life, but this seems to be far from the truth. Music has its own particular message for us and this message cannot be adequately interpreted through the medium of any other art.

The distinctive thing in music is sheer beauty of tone and tonal procedure. This should be kept definitely in mind during all rehearsals and concerts and every effort made to come

21

as nearly as possible to perfect attainment. For this purpose it is wise to include good music with simple technical demands which will permit concentration on the effort to secure as beautiful a performance as possible. This seems to me more truly educational than the development of prodigious technique.

A primary requisite of aesthetic enjoyment is auditory discrimination. Too often a musical performance consists only of the transition of impulses from eye to muscle. The cycle is not complete until the ear has registered and comprehended the result. It is therefore urgent that a certain section of each rehearsal be given over to music with slow movement, such as the Bach chorales. The performers must be intent upon hearing every tone and upon adjustment of individual intonation, so that the result may be as nearly perfect as possible. Strive always for beauty of tone and intonation. This point cannot be overemphasized.

Interpretive power is both mental and spiritual, although needing technical power for expression. Without a clear vision of the possibilities in a composition it is impossible to perform it in any way other than in a dull, uninteresting manner. Naturally the experience of the students has been limited and, if there is to be in their minds clear-cut images of interpretive values, it is necessary that the teacher accept the responsibility of inspiring the minds of these young people in such a way that the spirit of the music becomes a living thing demanding expression through their technical powers. My own experience with young people of high school age leads me to believe that the interpretive power of orchestras, bands, and choirs made up of these young people is limited to a very large extent by the interpretive powers of the instructors.

In order to assure that this interpretive power is present, I believe that school music teachers should have been, at one time or another, performers of high musical ability either vocally or upon some instrument. The orchestra and band director who is a "Jack of all trades" among musical instruments, but who has never mastered any particular one, can probably develop beginning bands in a somewhat satisfactory way; but beyond a certain point he no longer has the power to give the students the leadership they need and have every right to demand. It has been my misfortune to see more than one high school organization, capable of performing infinitely better than their actual performance, but who failed to progress because of an instructor who had reached the limit of his capacity and had no more to give them. What a tremendous loss to the young people in these organizations!

Social Values of Music. This is the second objective to be considered. It is of great importance, although not quite so much so as the aesthetic value. The rapid growth of school music in the public schools can be attributed largely to the fact that principals and superintendents everywhere have recognized its social value to the life of the school. This is especially true of the instrumental program and the band activity in particular. These administrators saw first of all its unifying effect upon school spirit through participation of music organizations in the auditorium, rallies, athletic games, community affairs, and other activities. Even though the educational value of the organization for its own members be questioned, the obvious result on the spirit of the school was sufficient, in the minds of many executives, to justify fostering the growth of these musical organizations in their schools.

The next important step in the recognition of social values was the discovery that these activities permitted growth in the capacity of the individual acting at the same time in a cooperative way towards a finished group product. Can there be any finer example of democratic organization? The student is permitted almost unlimited growth in his individual

23

powers and yet he is contributing his share according to his ability in the development of a unified whole. He receives respect for his offering to the common good and yet is made to realize that to make this activity complete he needs the help of others.

It is the belief in this second phase that makes possible the formation of an adequate school music program. Bands and orchestras were sufficient to stir school spirit, if able to play decently in tune and time. But for the development of the individual possessing talent but lacking training, it became necessary to form classes for the various instruments of the band and orchestra. Thus we provided for the development of the capacity of the individual, a capacity that is used later for service to the group as a whole. This idea applies equally to vocalists.

Technical Ability. The third major objective is technical ability. This is of primary importance to the aesthetic and social values. No matter what vision may be in the souls of the director and students in an aesthetic way, nor how strong their desire to carry on social projects, these are possible only in so far as their technique of performance permits. Therefore we must consider the development of technical powers.

Reference has been made in the discussion of aesthetic values to the necessity of developing beautiful tones and true intonation. Perhaps the strongest criticism that can be directed against school music group performance is that of poor tone and faulty intonation, so this deserves further consideration.

If a thoughtful selection of material has been made, it is perfectly possible to secure a high degree of success in both of these facets of performance. I fear that few school directors realize the worth of a very simple study for attaining these values. I am referring to the practice of using a hymn-like phrase—that is, with sustained tones in all parts—in which each chord is sounded as long as might be necessary to secure perfect intonation on the part of all. There is also a practice used by most of our best directors, which is to turn to the end of any selection that they desire to rehearse, asking the orchestra, band, or choir to play or sing the final chord and keep on sounding it, at the same time listening intently in order to discover and correct any fault of pitch. If this type of ear training is consistently followed over a long period of rehearsals, there will be a tremendous development in the accuracy of the ear which will translate itself into accuracy of intonation. This same idea may be used for drills in tone, attack and release, and dynamics.

It is a peculiar thing that many school music instructors, upon hearing a group play or sing in nearly perfect style, exclaim, "If only I had students who are as good as those!" In many cases they do have students as good or even better than those making up the organization they have just heard. The fault in their own group, in so far as technical ability is concerned, was largely that of overlooking tone development, phrasing, attack and release, and dynamics.

I have already referred to tonal development. In the matter of attack and release something more is necessary than drill. I am referring to the use of the baton by the director. It is amazing to realize how incompetent many music educators are with the baton. In the first place talent plays a large part in the use of the stick. Some people never will be able to use one easily. Others seem to pick it up naturally and rather quickly, but no one can handle a baton properly without a great deal of serious study under an instructor and by himself before a mirror. A baton rightly used has an almost magnetic ability to demand from performers the carrying out of the image in the conductor's mind. There should be a widespread movement to acquaint school musicians with the necessity for serious study in the use of the baton. Proper handling of the stick will do away with a large percentage of all technical problems in amateur groups. It is granted that certain intimate situations, or even the nature of certain selections, might prompt a director not to use a baton, but this in no way excuses him from the need of acquiring a baton technique.

It may seem that my discussion of the technical objective has been directed more to the instructor than to the student, but of course there are certain things that must be learned by the student. This the instructor cannot do for him. First of all, there should be maintained at all times the proper playing or singing position. Slovenly performance comes from slovenly habits, both mental and physical. The playing position required by many of the instruments is not a normal body position, but if consistent efforts are made always to hold to these forms they will become more and more natural to the performer and will eventually demand little or no conscious effort to maintain them. As I watch young people play I often notice how slowly their fingers react in the matter of stopping violin strings or pushing down valves. Consistent effort should be required, so that each movement is made in a clean-cut and decisive manner. In the matter of the strings, the result will be truer intonation and better tone; in the case of both strings and wind instruments, there will be more perfect rhythmical results. With vocal as well as with instrumental groups, the study of a true pianissimo helps greatly in both tone quality and steadiness of tone production.

So far I have not mentioned the study of rhythm except incidentally. However, rhythm is more or less the fundamental possession of every student and that which is needed to make this effective is proper attention to phrasing, attack and release, and dynamics. In listening to many school music groups perform such a rhythmical number as a march, we are often conscious of a steady rhythm, but the effect seems to be somewhat listless and heavy. This results from the fact that all beats or pulses are more or less similarly accented. A study of phrasing and the definite rhythmical patterns within a phrase will do a great deal towards correcting this fault. The students will grow to appreciate these rhythmical patterns if they are presented clearly enough to them and, when this is done, the music begins to take on a definite form. Lack of proper attack and release of both tones and phrases also is responsible for uncertain rhythmical feeling. It is usually quite easy to drill young musicians to attack properly; but release, even though just as important as attack, seems very difficult to secure even from many professional musicians. The study of dynamics will add the color necessary for the completion of the picture, in that it gives the needed highlights for interesting rhythmical form.

I have often used a plan with sturdy selections which I admit is open to criticism if used unwisely; but it undoubtedly secures results. This plan is the crowding of the beat just a shade without increasing the tempo. Very often the difference in the performance of a march by a professional and an amateur band is in just this little crowding of the beat, which gives to the one a feeling of energetic life and to the other a listlessness that makes the performance disappointing. This seems to place the performers on tiptoe and injects a distinct rhythm into the performance.

Of course, under this heading there is also the vast field of development of individual technique. This is important, but is concerned more with the technical growth of the individual than with the type of work taken up in ensemble groups in our schools. My object up to this point has been to make a few suggestions for the improvement of ensemble performance. These suggestions involve matters that are not as much emphasized in prevailing practice as they should be.

Secondary Objectives. There are some secondary objectives which merit brief consideration. The first is the growing need for vocational music courses in high schools,

27

especially in the larger cities. With the expansion of opportunities in American high schools there is still little chance
for the boy or girl expecting to enter the professional music
world to secure the drill work needed at that age without
sacrificing their general high school course. If a student is
attempting to carry on regular high school studies, the requirements are such that he finds too little time for the
proper development of his music. On the other hand, a
student devoted to music discovers that it is impossible to
maintain his required high school studies if he wishes to
keep up his music work, and he is forced to drop high
school. The result of this practice is very unsatisfactory. We
are constantly developing a large number of musicians without the academic training they should have and which by
right belongs to them. I often find that music programs are
slow in securing the necessary support because some music
educators are unable to talk the language of other people,
especially the administrators and general educators.

I want to tell of my experience with two boys who were
members of the Cleveland All-High School Orchestra a few
years ago. They had superior talent and had the definite intention of entering the professional music world. Through
great sacrifice, one of the boys was able to graduate from
high school in five years by taking extra work in two summer terms. The other boy found it impossible to keep up
the studies required by the school authorities and yet find
sufficient time to keep on properly with his musical training.
The result in this case was that the boy was lost to our
high school. The primary loss was to the second boy, for he
found himself more or less narrowly confined to musical
subjects alone. Both boys have become playing members of
the Cleveland Symphony Orchestra, one at twenty years of
age and the other at eighteen. This is one of many examples
that might be cited to show that very definite steps should
be taken in the school music program to provide for the

exceptionally talented. Through some type of vocational courses this could be accomplished.

It is not my thought to set up a purely technical music course for high school students in which they would be confined to intensive drill to prepare them for professional service. Instead, we should provide a wholesome balance of studies which will give students a fairly well-balanced knowledge of the world in which they live, and yet allow sufficient program time for music to provide for a steady development of powers along theoretical and applied music lines. The main objective would be to prevent students from becoming merely musical machines, no matter how perfect the working of that machine might be. Because the majority of professional work is done in the instrumental phase, it will be largely the duty of the instrumental teacher to set up the necessary program.

Development in the Instrumental Field. An articulated course in vocal and theoretical music is in effect, more or less, from the kindergarten to the high school. But instrumental teaching in many localities is rather fragmentary in that no continuous, well-organized course of study exists throughout all grades. Therefore it would seem wise that some additional thoughtful attention be given every program of instrumental study which should begin with the rhythmic orchestra of the kindergarten and culminate in senior high school ensembles of symphony proportions. This objective *is* attainable.

Everyone is familiar with the rhythmic orchestra for young children. It is very easy to introduce instruments of pitch gradually into this organization, as performers develop. The toy orchestra of the kindergarten should be continued in the first few grades, with the addition of melodic instruments (beginning in the third or fourth grades) and the elimination of more and more of the percussion instruments. Then pupils go to the elementary school orchestra.

During this process, every child should receive both opportunity and encouragement to study an instrument. It is not expected that all pupils will become performers, but there must be no neglect of talent or even interest in this field. From the seventh grade on, the present program of variously graded ensembles and instrumental classes should be continued and expanded when the need arises. This articulated instrumental program should in no way detract from nor compete with the continuing vocal program. Instead, if properly organized, it will become a contributing factor toward an integrated and comprehensive music education program.

The fact that school music instructors should first know clearly and definitely just what their objectives are should be emphasized again and again, and then, with the course set true, proceed to work as effectively as possible.

4

CREATIVE EXPERIENCES

IN MUSIC EDUCATION

"I feel that music has two definite phases, the creative and the appreciative. The creative may be the expression of original thought or the re-creation of an already recorded musical thought—in other words, the giving out of self. The appreciative is the understanding reception of another's message."

R.V.M.

Music educators are busy constantly with the re-creation of music in our singing and playing. That is an accepted activity in all public schools. We have not been so eager to agree that all humanity has creative power in varying degrees. Too often creativity has been left to the few, with the feeling that they only have this God-given power. That just isn't true. Everyone has composed a tune at some time or another. It may be only a fragment hummed or whistled and be unlovely to the listener, but it served to express some feeling close to the heart of the individual.

The creative approach in music education is for the purpose of vitalizing and making more significant the musical experience of every child. The essence of its purpose is the very opposite of formalized instruction and teacher-given information. The creative aspect of music education is not confined to the narrow objective of composing tunes or melodies, but concerns itself with every aspect of the developmental growth in music.

Creative Activities. A partial list of the types of creative activities would include:

1. Interpretation of musical compositions
2. Various experiences in rhythm or motion to music
3. Impersonation in the performance of songs
4. Dramatization
5. Development of singing games and folk dances in music
6. Addition of original stanzas to songs concerned with child activity
7. Selection of instrumentation for the rhythm band
8. Active listening which includes:
   a. Observation
   b. Comparison
   c. Discovery
   d. Discrimination
   e. Imagination
9. Creating harmonic background
10. Developing understanding of form through the composition of short songs and instrumental pieces

Each of these will be discussed in succeeding paragraphs.

Questions of Interpretation. Musical performance in the older type of instruction concerned itself with the mechanical devices of tempo, dynamics, and enunciation, rather than leading children to feel music within themselves and thereby discovering the proper basis for interpretation. Obviously, they will realize, if given a chance, that the lullaby should be sung or played in a soft and soothing manner and not with the strong decisive rhythm characteristic of a march. In the early stages, these questions of interpretation are extremely simple, but as the complexity and subtlety of music increase, so will discernment in the matter of mood and tempo. These decisions should be a joint matter for teacher and pupil rather than an imposition from a so-called musical authority.

Rhythm. The whole rhythmic program is essentially creative, as it brings into play free bodily responses to such things as pulse, accent, and rhythmic patterns. The term "motion to music" is an excellent expression of what is meant. There is also to be the development of mood feeling through rhythm and, of course, the story will have a great effect on rhythmic development. In the march rhythm, each pupil will try to develop the physical motions that obviously fit its expression. In the case of the minuet, a delicately pointed toe action will bring to children the character and quality of this musical form. As a matter of fact, the development of the simple basic step in every one of the dance forms will establish not only strength in rhythm, but contribute to the interpretation of music.

Dramatization. Impersonation provides an excellent avenue for understanding of music, but it must not be teacher imposed. In so far as possible, it should be the reaction of the child without a previously imposed conception on the part of the teacher. Dramatization is a more directly indicated impersonation. This might indicate that it applies only to song material, but great value can come from the development of the dramatic elements in instrumental music as well, and some forms of program music used in listening lessons can be equally stimulating.

Singing games and folk dances offer a great scope of creative experience and should be included in every music program. Many songs for small singers present a story concerning a series of incidents in child life, such as going to the store and visiting the zoo. It is possible to stimulate the musical reaction of children enormously by suggesting that they make up their own original stanzas on familiar topics. This would strengthen their understanding of rhythmic pattern and form structure and would also call for imagination.

The rhythm band probably has two primary purposes: first, the development of rhythmic power; and, second, the growing ability to discriminate in the choice of instruments appropriate to a given selection. There are many schools that think of this activity only as a performing body. In a sense, this is exploitation of the children and not an avenue of development. It is imposed upon children and they do as they are trained to do, which is a weak form of education. Bringing pupils into the center of the experience and stimulating their imagination in discovering what combinations of instruments best suit any particular piece of music is definitely valuable from the educational viewpoint. It is to be regretted that some situations ignore this procedure and drill for a perfect performance which is more for the entertainment of the school clientele than it is for child growth.

Listening—a Creative Process. Listening must be a creative process if it is to have any value. The faculty for observation must grow to the point where the child receives a clear-cut impression of the music he is hearing. He then must develop the power to compare music as it expresses mood, feeling, or emotion. The pupil then discovers what music says to him and begins to develop the power of judgment—that is, the making of a personal choice, which is a creative experience. Ultimately, all this increases the imaginative power of pupils, which is one of the outcomes in any program of music experience. Music listening is neither a static nor a passive activity; it must be one of great mental and emotional activity. If this is not so, the music is very apt to be just a pleasant sensory experience for the child and all of the significant factors of communication through patterns of tone are lost.

It is possible that many teachers feel that children hear

only melodies, but this is an entirely erroneous conception. Wherever there is melody, there is implied harmony; most pupils are sensitive to this feeling for harmonic background. Music education should help them discover simple harmonies for the melodies they know. This can be done in many ways. Some chords for small hands can be discovered through trial and error as a background for songs they love to sing. It is also possible for some of the pupils to make up another part for a melody, such as creating an alto part for a very familiar song. Even such social instruments as the harmonica, guitar, and accordion can be used in this activity, and the simple flute type of instrument can be used in making up other parts that would fit with some well-known melody. In the primary grades, when children are asked to make up a tune, teachers have discovered that certain harmonic backgrounds are acceptable to the children and other chord combinations are rejected because they are not in the mind or experience of the child. It is obvious that the pupil in the lower grades cannot write down the chords he wants or prefers. If the chords are heard in the mind, any other harmonic background is apt to be rather definitely refused when it differs from the child's original harmonic concept.

Writing Music. Now we come to an admittedly important phase of the creative program. That is the writing of songs and instrumental pieces. It must be remembered that the values in song creation lie not so much in the output as in the activity. The intrinsic value of the song is generally comparable to that of the child's English compositions, but the activity is tremendously worth while in its effect upon the child and upon his attitude towards music. First, there must be some idea as a basis for composition, then there must be the formation of a simple quatrain expressing the miniature story. Finding rhyming words proves to be an interesting activity for children.

Some underlying structure must be developed so that the

35

expression is rhythmical and produces a suitable lyric for musical composition. Then, various children can be asked to suggest tunes for the first phrase, the best one to be accepted by vote on the part of the children. While the teacher remains in the background to a large extent, her experience and training must furnish the necessary guidance and leadership wherever it is needed. Having completed the first phrase, we then meet the problem of musical form; that is, the type of second phrase that is suitable as a satisfactory reply to the first phrase. Care must be taken to see that there are compact and definite rhythmic patterns in the melody and that it doesn't wander off aimlessly into space. Then, by reference to songs they know and their familiar analysis of phrase A, phrase B, modified A, etc., the children can learn how to repeat a phrase to good advantage for the purpose of unity, and also to see the necessity of securing contrast by finding some other phrase that is different but yet seems to be a suitable response to the first phrase. This activity contributes greatly to an intelligent understanding of music, in that the children learn to see the necessity and value of form in music and begin to understand the way in which music is put together.

Basic Purpose of Creative Music. There is one great problem for creative education. As individuals become older, their critical faculties often cause them to reject their creative abilities as unsatisfactory. It is the belief of many that this is why the very obvious creative life of primary children atrophies, so that a pupil of junior or senior high school grade level will not attempt to express himself in an original composition. Overcoming this sensitivity is one of the great contributions a superior teacher can make. Some teachers object to this idea of composing melodies, saying that children cannot be expected to write good tunes. They forget that the purpose is not to develop a huge number of composers, but rather to have large numbers of our people understand the basic structure and composition of music. Creative experience will result in an understanding comparable to that gained through training in English composition, which enables children to understand and enjoy good writing as well as to develop an ability in written expression.

Finally, the true essence of art values in music are closely tied in with the creative program; and where such a program is not in operation, it is to be expected that the musical experience will be largely sterile and uninteresting. The primary purpose in music education is to have human beings thrill to the power and pleasure of music. To achieve this goal, music must become an avenue of expression and creative experience for every individual.

Again, the point needs to be made that the primary grades of American schools are, in the main, carrying on a very fruitful and valuable program of creative expression. It remains for music education to develop as significant and vital a program of creative music for those pupils in the upper elementary grades, the secondary schools, and our higher institutions of learning.

The two following quotations have afforded me a background for many hours of thought and, perhaps, will strengthen our individual creative attitude.

"For education consists not only in the possession of knowledge, but in the wisdom that may control, the courage and the skill to make the best of the knowledge we possess. . . . Behind the problem of diffusing knowledge lies the far greater problem of fitting men and women to possess knowledge and make a right use of it." [1]

"For the letter killeth, but the spirit giveth life."—II Corinthians, Verse 6.

[1] Dr. Lawrence Pearsall Jacks. Principal of Manchester College, University of Oxford.

The Creative Teacher

As the teacher is the key to this whole situation, it is necessary to consider the qualifications for one who is to assume this creative leadership. The following list is suggestive and not intended to be exhaustive.

1. Emotional power (to feel and express)
2. Discrimination and control
3. Ability to react clearly and intelligently to philosophies and psychologies
4. Musical intelligence
5. Accurate ear
6. Knowledge of what good tone really is
7. Leadership and agreeable personality
8. Showmanship
9. Ability to throw out non-essentials and concentrate on worth-while problems
10. Ability to sing and play the piano *artistically*
11. An insistent hunger for contact with good music
12. A huge enjoyment of life

Philosophies will and should differ with individuals, but no one may escape the necessity of teaching by some philosophy, even though done unconsciously. It is better to face this squarely and build an intelligent, clear, and consistent program of beliefs, rather than to drift and finally face disaster because the course has no fixed guide-lights.

Some of the problems we all need to face sooner or later are:

1. Music making as a craft and as an art
2. Analysis of musical talent
3. Social and art values in music

Russell V. Morgan served on the committee which wrote the "Statement of Beliefs and Purposes" for the Music Educators National Conference.

4. Dominance of emotional training over mental training in music education
5. Comparative weights of skills, knowledges, and appreciations
6. What is good music?

Objectives, to be valid, must have their foundations in whatever philosophies are sincerely accepted by the creative teacher. *Objectives* are frequently quite weak, either because they are so vague and all-inclusive as to defy specific treatment or because they consist of details raised to an attention wholly out of proportion to their worth. May I take the privilege of setting up five objectives which I believe a truly creative teacher could accept? The reader is invited to fire as critical a broadside as he desires. That is the way to discover weakness; but remember to criticise thoughtfully and without emotion.

1. A strong emotional and aesthetic response to music
2. A sense of freedom and exaltation after music experience
3. A pleasure and pride in ability to perform
4. An intelligent interest in the construction of music
5. Willingness to use talent for the enjoyment of others

Procedure is our plan of attaining the objectives that were determined as desirable in the light of our philosophy. Our work is done on shifting sand if our procedure is not developed in this manner. Everything done should be tested in the light of what is considered to be basic values.

Materials and Equipment. Just two brief statements will suffice here. Musical material must first of all pass the test of artistic worth. Nothing less than good is acceptable. This does not mean difficult music, as some of the greatest works are simple, technically.

Equipment must be at hand which will give musical at-

39

mosphere. Poor equipment means a serious handicap and sometimes positive harm. Extrinsic helps are never to be overlooked.

Permanent Values

The term "residue" has been used by general educators to indicate that which remains with the individual after any type of experience. This is a thought-provoking subject and should be pondered by all music educators.

There is value in passing or fleeting enjoyment, if it is not destructive; but the "residue," in terms of attitudes, knowledges, skills, etc., is the true permanent value. Careful study should be given to determine to some extent the actual "residue" value of our musical education.

A creative attitude helps make a creative teacher and the teaching done by this person will produce a desirable "residue."

5

LISTENING

"One important phase of education is, without doubt, a development of many and varied appreciations. We are chiefly concerned in music with the development of an aesthetic appreciation beyond the power of words to express or the mind to translate into definite thoughts. There is a hunger in every man for just this thing, whether he knows it or not, and the bitterness and hopelessness of many lives could have been relieved or prevented if a proper introduction had been given to the power of the arts to elevate one above material things."

R.V.M.

The amount of music being poured into American ears by radio, television, sound pictures, and recordings would seem to be more than could be assimilated; but the fact that attendance at musical programs has increased to a striking degree seems to indicate that the flood of music with which we are now coming in contact only whets the appetite for more. This obvious increase in musical desire and enjoyment has influenced both the community and the school in their attitude toward the position of this art as part of the educational program. If so many people have

41

such a strong liking for music, it seems to be the responsibility of education to help students increase their ability to enjoy more fully these musical offerings.

All Music Courses as Music Appreciation. Every human being likes music and differences exist only in the kind of music chosen, so that the problem for the school is first to discover and use as a contact that particular responsive level on which each individual finds himself and then to provide a cumulative and developing program which will help him reach his highest level of reception and understanding. It is not easy to discover that responsive level of the individual and perhaps a great deal of blundering has occurred in our attempt to find music material and musical activities that will seem significant, interesting, and worth while to the various students in our schools. Teachers differ in their ideas of approach to the student. Some feel that the introduction should be made through popular music with which the student is best acquainted, while others feel that only the very highest quality of music can be justified in an educational program. It would appear that a little search and care would discover for us light music of real quality which would serve as the introductory phase and which would normally lead to a liking for heavier music later.

The term "music appreciation" was formerly used in a very restricted sense to indicate a program which included only listening materials and some extrinsic information. It is true that the proponents of this activity urged the necessity of securing active listening and warned against the danger that would result where a passive attitude was permitted. Other members of our profession have constantly felt that such a narrow interpretation of music appreciation would, in the end, defeat our whole purpose and have had a strong desire to integrate participation and listening.

I feel that music appreciation is one of the ultimate goals of all music instruction in schools, and that every course—

whether it deals with vocal or instrumental music, with theory, history, or with so-called music appreciation—demands some degree of active participation in order to motivate and stimulate growth in musical understanding. The belief should be emphasized that every chorus teacher, every band and orchestra instructor, and every grade music teacher is definitely engaged in a program of appreciation. It is true that these teachers must concern themselves with the development of performing skills; but, in the final analysis, skills are always a means to an end and seldom worthy of serious general educational acceptance if isolated.

Training of the Ear

The fundamental phase of music education which underlies every variety of course is training of the ear; again, not primarily as a skill, but as a means of securing sharply focused impressions as the basis for aesthetic enjoyment. The purpose of ear training in music education is three-fold: *first*, to develop sensitivity to musical sound; *second*, to insure growth of comprehension of significant combinations of sound; and, *third*, to develop the power of retention—that is, the ability to retain mentally a series of tonal and rhythmic patterns so that they take on musical meaning. The abilities listed here might be called "tool equipment" for any musical listener. His power to enjoy and understand music will depend upon the keenness and sureness of this physical-mental equipment. On the development of these abilities will depend the listener's power to progress from the simple recognition of a short tune to the much more demanding equipment needed to understand clearly the complex weaving of tonal and rhythmic patterns present in a symphony or tone poem. The extent to which these abilities may be developed rests upon certain native capacities.

Many of us are only partly conscious of the musical sounds which surround us, and it seems that our first responsibility is to develop a keen awareness and power of concentration directed towards such sounds. The capacity of individuals will vary in this regard, but all subsequent development must necessarily be conditioned by the degree to which we have been able to develop this sensitivity to musical tones. In the second place, through organized instruction, we must reach higher levels of comprehension of the musical patterns, both tonal and rhythmic. Beautiful musical sounds, each independent of the other, can never create music. It is only as we understand the forward flow and structural significance contained in the patterns of these sounds that we have a basis for true musical hearing. These first two steps are usually taken care of in the teaching of music, but our next step is rarely given the importance it deserves. This final step, the power of retention of musical patterns, is extremely important. Only in so far as we are able to retain in our minds the significant structure of music, as it unfolds itself to our ears, are we able to properly receive the larger forms of musical composition. Therefore, the necessity for development of the retentive power just discussed must be particularly emphasized.

This view of appreciation should sweep away that perplexity which so many people have concerning the differences between enjoyment of music and all this business of technical preparation which sometimes seems to point the opposite way from true enjoyment. There is a distinct need for music appreciation classes for the many boys and girls who at present find no place in the applied music groups and yet possess a justifiable craving for some contact with music. There is no conflict in this broad picture.

Concert Music to Widen Experiences

A highly significant phase which deserves more emphasis is that of concerts specially designed for child audiences. *Types of Concerts.* Concerts for children fall into two divisions; *first*, programs presented within the individual schools by soloists and small ensembles of artists; and *second*, performances given by large professional groups, such as choral organizations and symphony orchestras, housed in a central concert hall to which the boys and girls are transported from various schools. Each type of activity is valuable but it is obvious that many communities are not in a position to offer "live" orchestral concerts. It is possible, however, for many schools to present a well-thought-out series of concerts by soloists and small ensembles.

Purpose of These Programs. In my judgment, there are two highly important purposes for concerts for children. In the first place, the children come in contact with a vastly wider field of musical literature and, in the second instance, they hear and see a performance possessing artistic qualities of a high order.

If musical experience is to be confined to songs that boys and girls can sing in the classroom, two weaknesses are immediately apparent. There are many songs which students may enjoy and appreciate that possess technical difficulties too great for their mastery in performance. A wealth of musical stimulation is denied the child who may hear only those songs which he himself can sing. Then, too, the whole library of instrumental music is closed to him.

The loveliness of music cannot be realized for most of us except through its interpretation by a fine artist. After all, notation is a mere suggestion of the musical idea and accurate reproduction of the indicated duration and pitch does not insure perfect reproduction of the music. As we hear a beautiful interpretation, we become increasingly sensitive to enriched musical values. These values cannot be expressed in words nor in musical notation, but, nevertheless, constitute the reality of the art. It is the experiencing of the beauty in music that stimulates and quickens our own musical imagination to the point where we can more clearly

45

discern the aesthetic qualities in any composition. Many of us can testify to the increased awareness of musical beauties that follows the hearing of a superb artist.

Concert attendance should be considered as a musical excursion or perhaps as a laboratory where the students glimpse a realm of beauty which up to this time was totally unknown. The value of these concert performances lies in their capacity to increase sensitivity to aesthetic qualities and to stimulate our search through and beyond mere musical notation to the true musical expression.

The Material Used at Concerts. The material used at concerts must be of high quality. Boys and girls have an uncanny sense for detecting shoddy and meaningless things in art. They also sense and respect beauty even in compositions that in some ways seem too complicated or subtle for them. Occasionally, well-meaning people point out the fact that certain numbers have implications that are "over the heads" of young listeners. Perfectly true; but, so long as musical beauty is present in abundance, there is every reason to feel justified in using such music. Our fault in this field is usually to aim too low rather than too high. After all, truly great art has a directness and simplicity that captures children. The problem here is not so much over-reaching in the selection of material as it is the failure to provide a truly adequate and artistic performance.

Preparation before the Concert. Adequate preparation before attending a concert is essential. A tragic mistake of earlier years was that of forcing children to sit through a concert for which they were in no way prepared to listen. Even the trained music critic confesses that his first hearing of many compositions results in confused impressions. Music possesses highly organized form and structure, but this is not apparent until musical memory has been developed to the point of retaining at least some comprehension of the composition as a whole. Naturally, a part of the preparation for concert attendance should be careful listening to recordings of as much of the material as is available.

It is worth while to know at least something of the human side of the composer, because our feelings towards his music seems warmer if we think of him as a person—as one of us. Then we should know something of the story connected with the music if it has a *real* story, and some realization of the form or structure, so that it is intelligible to us. But, above all, insist upon sufficient hearing of the recording so that the concert performance will give the children the feeling of welcoming an old friend. This preliminary preparation actually produces results, and that is more than can be said of the verbose and endless "explanatory" remarks which so many artists make to children.

To function properly, the preparation periods and the concert attendance must integrate with the regular music class work. Too often a feeling prevails that the concert is totally unconnected with the school curriculum and that there is a lack of the stimulation that should be carried back to the classroom and expressed in deeper musical feeling. Proper and thorough preparation causes concert attendance to be a thrilling occasion. In turn the concert should result in a strong desire on the part of the children to express some of this same musical beauty in their own classrooms.

Teaching of Listening and the History of Music

Approximately thirty per cent of the young people in the secondary schools of America are enrolled in some type of musical activity. The question naturally arises, what about the remaining seventy per cent? It would seem logical that a certain proportion of this seventy per cent, at least, would have some interest in music from the audience standpoint.

If we think only of this general group of students at the high school level, and not of the smaller groups who are actively engaged in music, two questions arise: (1) What type of instruction will best meet the needs of this general student? (2) What qualifications should be possessed by the faculty members who present such a course?

The Need of the General Student. Many young people in this group have a desire to be a little more intelligent about and acquainted with music, but the type of instruction which they have met does not always seem to be headed in the direction of their interests. What they need most of all is a close contact with music itself, with compositions which have been carefully selected for the purpose of arousing interest and satisfying a desire for music. Then there must be a certain amount of historical background and simple presentation of the various forms in music, so that the students may have something specific and definite for which to listen. Many general students need to have certain extrinsic materials presented to them, in order to arouse their curiosity and interest. Ultimately their attention can be concentrated upon the music itself. If we can secure concentration and active listening, then the music will carry over its intrinsic values to its young listeners.

The Faculty for Such a Course. Most important of all, the teacher needs to have both a contagious enthusiasm for music and a sufficient historical background in order to select basic values for presentation. With this proper background a great deal of extraneous matter will not be permitted to come between the pupil and the music. The teacher should be thoroughly trained in musicianship and should have an acquaintance with an enormous amount of music literature plus the ability to present selections at the piano keyboard. All of this must be present plus a contagious personality for success in this field.

As a last thought on listening to music, let me remind you that everyone is a listener, whether it be done voluntarily or involuntarily, so let us be alert and intelligent about it.

6

MUSICAL PERCEPTION

"How wonderful and significant it would be to develop in our students the power of musical perception which would unfold to them year after year the musical beauties of the masters, supplementing and strengthening their own growing capacity for self-expression."

R.V.M.

The term "musical perception," as used here, refers to the process of acquiring an accurate mental image of a musical composition. This image, once acquired, is referred to as a concept. A concept embraces melody, harmony, rhythm, form, beauty of tone, and interpretation. A concept of these elements is foundational in building thorough musical understanding on the part of all students. As this phase of music education is either omitted or avoided by most school music teachers, let us try to discover its relationship to musical performance; that is, whether it is incidental to rehearsals and performance or whether it is a distinct phase of musical training calling for a definite plan of procedure not necessarily included in routine drill.

Types of Musical Concepts. There is a challenge for thought in the fact that a considerable number of performers are not musicians at all, but musical mechanics. This is especially true of some instrumentalists. It is not unusual to find students who have developed a truly remarkable ability to translate eye impressions into muscular activity, without being conscious of an auditory image. Yet the auditory image is fundamental to the development of a true musician, and performance is intelligent only to the degree that the performer is acutely conscious of this mental picture of the music. Musical conception, then, is an essential part of the equipment of every musician and it is wise for every school music instructor to give thoughtful attention to the procedure for securing this necessary attribute; in other words, a method for developing the power of musical perception.

As has been indicated elsewhere, I believe that a certain portion of every rehearsal period should be given over to the playing or singing of easy, slow-moving music of the choral type, in which every participant has ample time to become conscious not only of his own part, but of each chord being sounded by the entire ensemble. The value of this training lies in the fact that the student is receiving a full harmonic concept and is consequently much better able to secure perfect intonation in his own part, while, at the same time, he is acquiring a much broader appreciation of the beauty in the music. It follows that the individual musical output will become an intelligent contribution to a complete art work.

The phase of musical perception just mentioned, however, has to do only with the perpendicular element in music. Subsequent repetitions should bring to the student a conscious appreciation and understanding of the melodic flow of parts other than his own. It is only through a clear concept of the musical values of the other parts that a performer can best make his own singing or playing an integral part of the composition. Nuances and the "tossing of dialogue" back and forth between various instruments or voice parts thus become much more significant. Appreciation of such effects contributes to an exaltation of spiritual feeling otherwise denied the performer.

Still more experience with a chorale will permit the student to discover a lovely balance of the phrase—the first step in the long, hard road to adequate perception of form. The next step is comparatively easy, being an awakening of a consciousness of the way in which one phrase is supplemented and balanced by another. Clear perception of the musical balance between two phrases will provide the groundwork for a more extended study of form. Someone has compared the form of music to the drawing of a beautiful picture with a luminous point, the lines disappearing as rapidly as formed. The only possible conception of such a picture would be in the retention by the mind of each part, the completed work being purely a mental image. Perception, or the ability to build a concept from such an act, will depend upon clear impressions consciously retained. This is a very difficult thing to do.

A performance of music is never easy to listen to unless the rhythmical pattern or framework is clearly set forth and, until the performer has a clear image in his mind of the ebb and flow of rhythm, he cannot hope to offer an intelligent performance to the auditor. Rhythm is eventually a matter of the mind, and physical rhythmic motion is valueless except in so far as it is actually controlled by a clear mental concept.

Beauty of tone must be foremost in the mind of the student. In passing, it might be wise to say that it should be the insistent demand of everyone, performers and listeners alike. Beauty of tone can only be secured by having a concept of lovely tone always in mind. The finest presentation comes as a result of beautiful mental singing. This is true whether the music is vocal or instrumental, for without a song in the heart there can be no loveliness of tone.

Interpretation depends first upon a concept that is clean-cut in all details. Having made the image of a composition part of one's self, freedom begins. By this is meant the fact that only halting utterance can be given a musical message when the performer has no conception of the composition as a whole and is conscious only of notes—one by one—as he actually produces them. It is wise, therefore, to make every effort to help the student to build up, mentally, as complete a picture as possible. Having secured this, there comes the task of persuading him to release his personality, his whole being, if you please, in an art expression.

The Power of Self-Expression. There is in the American youth an unbounded energy calling for some kind of self-expression. This expression of self must and will find ways of venting its vital force, so the question is how best to use it. Shall it be manifested in ways contrary to the best good of the social life of the community or shall it be used in activities contributing to the growth of the best side of the individual and to the members of the community of which the individual is a part? There can be no indecision here.

It seems pertinent at this place to suggest thoughtful consideration of two types of interest, mechanical and musical. I am convinced that joy in the mechanical manipulation of an instrument is many times mistaken for real musical interest. The two interests cannot be wholly separated, as nearly everyone has some love for music tucked away in his being. It is simply a question as to which interest dominates.

With some hesitation the theory is advanced that people with mechanical talent find that the playing of an instrument offers an easy expression for a comparatively small musical urge, and that sincere joy in music is often denied expression to others who have little or no mechanical ability. This would seem to call for a rather careful appraisal of our music education activities to discover how much of our work is mechanical and how much is musical.

Mechanical talent is precious and is essential to free and

satisfying self-expression, but after all it is only a tool that is to a certain degree necessary in the production of a musical art work that is in itself a more or less beautiful flowering of a personality. In America, we can say with just pride that our music is making surprising strides in technical proficiency, but I must, in all sincerity, raise a question concerning an equal development of the sort of musical ability which demonstrates true musical perception.

Functioning Perceptive Power. A short experience with two or three bands and orchestras in small cities in Europe proved rather illuminating to me. Faulty technique and bad instruments marked the production of some musical performances that would not be tolerated by the musical directors of our better school orchestras, and yet both performers and hearers were aroused to a point of musical enthusiasm hard to describe. How could this happen? In America, that concert hall would have been quickly emptied and the auditors would wait until next month when the finest orchestra in the world was to perform, or perhaps it would be the greatest pianist or the greatest violinist. What is the attitude of mind that causes this contrast? We cannot believe that it is because we are the only people really to appreciate good music.

My theory concerning this differing response is that the auditors of the European orchestras mentioned before had made that potentially lovely music such a part of themselves that even a faulty performance brought to them a mental image or concept that was limited in its loveliness only by the perceptive power and rich emotional life of the individual.

How wonderful and significant it would be to develop in our students the power of musical perception which would unfold to them year after year the musical beauties of the masters, supplementing and strengthening their own growing capacity for self-expression.

53

7

RADIO — ITS CONTRIBUTION

TO MUSIC EDUCATION

"The craftsmanship may be perfect, but real greatness will be found in the realm of the artistic if the product is to be significant."

R.V.M.

Radio has had an enormous influence upon the cultural life of all American citizens. With receiving instruments in the majority of homes, a flood of programs offering music, drama, comedy skits, and serious talks have come to the ears of young and old. Each one of us has a wide choice in the radio programs to which we listen. The majority of listeners seem to prefer music. This explains why approximately eighty per cent of all present broadcasts are either music or related to music. Among the musical offerings there is again need for choice and, while a large number desire light music, there is a steadily growing audience for the more serious musical offerings. This comparatively new force in American life and the still newer force of television has brought lovely music, beautifully performed, to millions of our people who otherwise would never know such musical experiences. Within three decades we have progressed from a land of "music for the few" to a country of "music for all." The radio affords universal opportunity for music education in its broadest sense and the potentialities of television seem almost limitless.

The Beginning. Our country has recognized the educational power of radio from its inception and has insisted that every radio station devote a certain portion of its time on the air to public service programs. In meeting this requirement, many stations have turned to educators for guidance. While considerable cooperation is evident, it is surprising that commercial stations have met with some indifference and even some antagonism. At present, the majority of educational programs available from commercial stations fit into three categories: (1) listening programs for schools, (2) programs designed for children as they listen in their homes, and (3) music programs by school students.

A few educational institutions accepted the challenge seriously and it is upon the slow and difficult experiences of this early group that the recent expansion of educational broadcasting is based. Music for the listener was the first type of program developed. However, it had all the advantages and disadvantages of the old record-playing music appreciation lesson.

It was not long before experimentation took place in the field of direct instruction in singing and playing. In spite of mistakes and flaws, the real values of music education by radio became more and more apparent. Some influential educators became convinced that broadcast music lessons could improve the quality of learning and it was their enthusiasm and determination that broke through the inertia which had seemed to place education in chains as far as radio was concerned.

Educational Radio Stations. The development of FM (frequency modulation), using high frequencies assigned specifically to non-commercial uses by our government, opened the door for further development of educational broadcasting and the building of radio stations by schools, colleges and universities, and state departments of education—these to be operated entirely for educational purposes. Thus the educational broadcasters were freed from some of the regulations and restrictions which had hampered educational programs over commercial stations, such as rigid time schedules, the need for continuous sound, and the highly entertaining but wasteful type of script. The U.S. Office of Education recognized the values of education by radio and engaged a Chief of Radio to function within the department.

With all this, very few educational stations were built and there came a time in 1946 when the FCC (Federal Communications Commission) thought seriously of abandoning a segment of these non-commercial airways that had been reserved for educational use because of the small number of schools asking for assignments. A strong interest was quickly manifested in all parts of the country and schools which had received assignments between 1940 and 1945 began immediately to build stations and develop the necessary personnel for effective operation.

The Radio Lesson

As school systems build their own stations, there will be expanding opportunities to enter the field of direct music instruction by radio on all grade levels. Programs for the first six grades are tremendously important; experience has proved that radio lessons directed to pupils in these grades are especially successful in the fields of rhythmic activity, art rote songs, song study, and listening lessons. The radio script for this instruction can be prepared by a master teacher and broadcast directly to a specific grade level in such a way as to assist the classroom teacher greatly in the lesson and in the general quality of the music teaching.

Preparation and Production. In preparing and producing the radio lessons for direct classroom use, it is understood that they become a part of the basic course in music education and that the scripts are prepared by expert teachers and produced with the services of excellent singers, instrumentalists, and speakers. The classroom teacher has a direct responsibility for preparing the class to receive the lesson, for having all needed materials available to the children, and for whatever follow-up is deemed desirable.

Rhythmic Activities. Radio lessons which involve rhythmic activities can be taught in a very successful manner. A perfect performance, with strong rhythmic swing, possible only when given by an expert performer, comes directly to each classroom. This is of great assistance to the teacher and provides an exciting learning experience for the child. Teachers welcome this type of lesson, particularly in view of the limited time they have available for preparation and, in many cases, because they feel limited, technically.

Rote Songs. Songs of all types, from the simple sentence song to the difficult art song, can be successfully presented by radio. These songs can be brought to the classroom in the most perfect performance possible, both as regards voice and accompaniment. Expert methods of presentation can be used. Here again, the classroom teacher has a very important place in preparation and follow-up.

Song Study. Radio lessons in song study for those grades involved with the processes of note reading have been very successful. The script should be a carefully prepared model or demonstration lesson, written by an expert in the music teaching field who is efficient in developing the study items without waste of time or motion. Here again, as in other types of lessons, there should be an understanding that this is a part of the basic music education curriculum and is sent as a help to the teacher, who remains in the center of the teaching picture and who will be needed for subsequent

57

class activity. It has been demonstrated successfully that all problems involved in reading music can be taught effectively through the use of radio lessons.

Young Listeners. Programs of music for young listeners are particularly useful. It is possible to present the finest music, selected for interest appeal to children of specific grade levels. This music, whether recorded or "live," should be presented by outstanding performers.

SUPPLEMENTARY USE OF RADIO

In addition to regular lessons as part of the basic music curriculum, many valuable supplementary activities are possible through the use of radio. Success has been demonstrated in the areas described in the following paragraphs.

Programs by Student Groups. Special emphasis and correlation may be given through programs based on a special theme and presented by student groups. This is an incentive for perfection of performance and aids in establishing performance standards over a large area. These broadcasts may involve music of different nations represented in the American citizenry; music of the New World, which would include songs and instrumental selections of our neighbors both north and south; early American music; music by American composers; etc.

Supervision. School-operated radio stations can save a great deal of time and energy by making it possible for supervisors and administrators to talk directly to teachers in various buildings, thereby saving the travel necessary when a faculty meeting is called for a central place.

Testing. The radio affords an unusual opportunity for presenting a uniform testing program. This method has proven equally successful with both aptitude music tests and with tests of musical accomplishment. Tests given by radio can be presented simultaneously and efficiently to a very large number of students. There is the advantage of absolute uniformity of administration as well as the advantage of offering the test without the paraphernalia preventing the student from concentrating upon the test itself.

If the instructions and the test are both recorded before the broadcast, every student will receive exactly the same presentation of the test, thus removing the question of variation which occurs when the tests are administered in individual classrooms by numerous teachers.

It is also feasible to present diagnostic tests by radio which will help the teacher evaluate the work covered by the students, so that special help may be given where weaknesses are shown. Achievement tests uniformly administered will enable the teacher to judge the progress and standing of individual pupils against established norms.

Tests which disclose indication of native music ability have been given to junior and senior high school pupils by radio and used in guiding these pupils into music activities where probable success will be greatest. In some cases these tests have been used in the upper elementary grades with considerable success.

Summary. There are three major categories of music programs which may be presented by radio for school use: (1) programs especially written and produced by a school staff, (2) programs written and produced by a commercial staff, and (3) sustaining programs.

All types of radio programs in music education may be grouped into four classifications: (1) basic music instruction, (2) supplementary music instruction, (3) promotional, and (4) recreational.

The specific purposes of radio programs for music education are (1) to improve skills and techniques, (2) illustrations to establish concepts of acceptable interpretation and tone quality, (3) appreciation, (4) recreation, and (5) leisure.

SUPERVISORY STANDPOINT. Some of the many supervisory

and administrative values afforded by radio: (1) It presents to the teacher a perfectly made and expertly given lesson which cannot help but serve as a model in the teacher's organization of her own lessons, (2) It provides real assistance to the teacher in proper organization of materials, both through the preparatory instructions and the follow-up, (3) Develops an excellent example of cooperation between supervision and the classroom, (4) Gives a natural uniformity of instruction, (5) Multiplies many times the coverage of supervision, and (6) Has a high musical value in respect to choice of material, tone quality, and interpretation of songs.

TEACHING STANDPOINT. Teachers are enthusiastic because of the things they can accomplish through music lessons by radio: (1) They offer highly expert instruction directly to the child, (2) Bring to each classroom the stimulation and guidance of an excellent singing voice, (3) Make available to every classroom a piano accompaniment which completes the musical message of the song, (4) Make it possible to introduce other instruments which enrich the musical values of the lesson in a way impossible to each classroom teacher without the radio, (5) Develop a high degree of concentration because of the uninterrupted movement of the radio lesson, (6) Bring to the teaching program an enrichment and background that would be impossible for individual teachers to attain, and (7) Help to secure patent cooperation, because homes are made acquainted with the purpose and type of music education offered in the school.

PUPIL'S STANDPOINT. They learn and like it!

GOING ON THE AIR

There are a few problems outstanding in the experience of every school group which attempts to place its performance on the air waves. The following statements about going on the air with school or amateur groups may seem obvious and commonplace, but a great deal of experience convinces me that the everyday problems here presented must be solved anew with each attempt to broadcast.

One difficulty is in the attempt to obtain objective evaluation in connection with a performance. Usually, instructors and friends are so wrapped up in good wishes for the group that they find it difficult to apply critical analyses to the actual performance of the student group. This is only natural, but it is one of the biggest pitfalls that faces us in our broadcasts by school musicians. One way of achieving an objective evaluation is to record the program some time previous to the broadcast date and to study it carefully. Through this medium it is possible for both teachers and students to become more critical, in a constructive way, of their own performance. This is a device which should become more and more common as music educators understand its value. Could it be that musical directors are fearful of "hearing themselves as others hear them," in this objective and impersonal manner?

A second item in this objective evaluation is the necessity for "monitoring" the program previous to the broadcast. Perhaps the greatest good comes from this monitoring when it is possible to have such expert checking at the station a week prior to the broadcast, to be followed by a final monitoring an hour before the group goes on the air. Problems in balance and in tone quality will show up strikingly in a monitor hearing and, by having some time for work at school following this first hearing, it is possible to eliminate these difficulties to a great degree and thus leave the final monitoring on the day of the broadcast for the relatively easy matters of distance and direction of the microphone, placement of individuals, etc.—a last-minute smoothing up process.

A third major item in this objective evaluation is to study audience interest as it touches a given radio program. The total area of audience interest resides in sound, and all critical objective evaluation must be confined to sound alone.

Suggestions. A few thoughts concerning the actual broadcasting period may be helpful. As a musical group performs in an auditorium for a seated audience, the air waves generated in the singing or playing will smooth more and more as they travel a longer distance. However, in a broadcasting studio, every sound that goes on the air is gathered up at one focal point—the microphone—and the only thing that any listener can hear will be the exact reproduction of the sound as it exists at the one place the microphone stands. With radio, there is only one distance and that is from the performing group to the microphone and, when sound reaches the microphone, it is just as though the sound were set in concrete, with every flaw fixed tightly and carried exactly that way to all listeners. In checking a group for broadcasting, the director who is listening objectively should stand in the exact position in which the microphone is to be placed. By closing one ear tightly, the resultant sound will be astonishingly close to that which would come over the radio. After listening to the group in this way, a director is not so prone to repeat a frequently heard statement to the effect that the microphone distorts the efforts of school musicians. This really is not true, for it merely records exactly the sound that exists at a certain given point.

Intonation is one of the real problems in broadcasting. Even the finest professionals have a slight variation of pitch in a unison tone and, of course, in amateur groups that variation or band, as we might term it, is even wider. Every effort must be made to reduce the width of this band so that each voice or instrument is as close to the center of true intonation as is possible. Otherwise the resultant sound from the radio will be rather distressing.

In the placing of groups it is well to remember the danger of echoes from other walls in the studio. There is also the necessity for enough space so that the tones may speak freely and easily. Some best results come from placing a chorus facing toward a wall, but perhaps eight or ten feet away from it. With the microphone close to the wall and drapes or other good sound-absorbent material back of it, a resonance and clarity can be achieved that is quite complimentary to the group. In the matter of instrumental organizations, it is usually much simpler to place them before the microphone, as every studio producer does who has had a great deal of experience in this field. However, it probably will be necessary to move certain players closer to the microphone and certain other instruments further away. Unless your school band or orchestra has had the opportunity to rehearse with this changed set-up, they will be somewhat confused by the different direction from which the various sounds come and the resulting discomfort will tend to lower the quality of the broadcast. It is suggested, therefore, that any instrumental group preparing for a broadcast learn to adjust itself to changes in seating plan. However, the use of multiple microphones and multiple-direction microphones can eliminate the need for some of this adjustment in placement.

It is usually helpful to have a blackboard in full view of the performers which lists the titles of the selections, in the order in which they are to be performed. No sheets of paper should be used to give this schedule because of the risk of the rattle being conveyed over the radio. Also, this blackboard presentation of the program makes each student an intelligent unit in carrying out the successive numbers.

Another point of importance is to study the time and tempo of each number so that the conductor may have on his stand a schedule which shows the playing time of each number and the exact time within the complete broadcasting schedule when each number is to be finished. This enables the conductor to know instantly whether he is fifteen seconds behind or thirty seconds ahead of time, and he can therefore adjust the timing of the numbers to follow. In spite of the best plans, tempos of numbers will vary slightly and the director may find himself approaching the end of a program with a minute to spare. To take care of this, it is suggested that the director always have at hand a simple, short number to be hummed by vocal groups or played by the strings in the orchestral groups, or woodwinds in the case of bands, which can take the group on the air, during the introduction, and can be used as filler at the end of the program if needed. It is possible to start right out in this signature number with full tone and then, when the time comes for the announcer to make his final statement, the musical group can be "faded out" and sound quite professional in its closing moments.

The use of unusually large or massed groups for broadcasts presents additional problems. Beyond a certain point, every individual added to any part, either in vocal or instrumental groups, becomes a liability, in that each added performer broadens the band of intonation and blunts the point of rhythmic beats so that the result is confused and lacks the clarity which is so essential in good broadcasting.

Many schools today have recording machines and school broadcasting equipment, so that it is possible to develop a definite evaluation of a performance without leaving the school building. A real study of the points mentioned here should make it possible for directors to be proud of the performances given by their school groups. The necessity for objective evaluation of each performance should be mentioned again and again, otherwise going on the air may result only in distress to the director and friends of the school.

Radio Production as a Classroom Project

Most elementary school children get a real thrill from pretending they are giving a radio broadcast. They hear many programs and have very good ideas of how they want their own program organized. As teachers are not always quite sure how to approach this project some suggestions may be helpful.

Organization. The members of the class will need to be organized into groups or committees to work in the following areas:

1. RESEARCH COMMITTEE to agree on a topic or theme for the broadcast and present this to the class for approval and suggestions. This committee supplies the information needed by the committee which will do the writing of the script.
2. SCRIPT COMMITTEE to prepare the script and submit it to the class for suggestions. Responsibility for the exact wording of what is to be said, as well as the exact timing of all items contained in the script, belongs to this committee.
3. MUSIC COMMITTEE to select all music material to be used. The songs and instrumental numbers must be suitable to the theme.
4. PRODUCTION COMMITTEE to be responsible for all equipment, including sound effects. This committee selects and rehearses the performers and is charged with making the production run smoothly.

Vocabulary. Certain terms are used in professional broadcasting and children should know their meaning and use them in conversation. Examples follow:

1. SCRIPT—the written program or continuity which contains all the spoken words and indicates the places for music, sound effects, etc.
2. CUE—the signal given a performer, or group of performers when his part is to start. This is usually done by pointing.

3. SOUND EFFECTS—these must be appropriate to the mood and should never detract from what is being said nor the music being performed. They are used to give realism to the program.

4. FADE—literally means to become softer. To "fade under" means to continue softly after fading while words are being spoken. To "fade out" means to continue growing softer until the sound is gone entirely.

As more school systems build their own FM educational stations, many of these classroom radio production projects can be put on the air to serve as increased motivation for the children and as a public relations activity between school and the community.

TELEVISION

The advent and widespread use of television has tended to enhance all of the educational values of radio and has added the visual avenue. Telecasting techniques which in many respects are similar to broadcasting will need careful study by music educators and school stations so that programs involving participation by school musicians will portray accurately the music education which is available to all the children of all the people of our country. There should be no avoidance nor lessening of standards but rather a sincere effort to make our contribution to music education through this powerful medium equally powerful.

8

MUSIC IN THE
CLEVELAND SCHOOLS

"Possession of song books and musical instruments will not make America musical; but a great joy in the intimate, personal possession of musical power offers the pathway to our hope of making American lives richer and happier."
R.V.M.

In 1846, the Cleveland Board of Education established music classes among the basic required courses for the education of Cleveland children. The development of a sense of beauty thus became one of the primary purposes of education and established the opportunity for growth in aesthetic, emotional, and spiritual responses.

It is the purpose of music education to bring to each child the maximum musical enjoyment of which he is capable. Technical instruction in music is used for the purpose of reaching this maximum and is not considered an end in itself. Wherever such technical instruction will increase musical ability it has a place in education. Listening lessons, rhythmic activities, song singing, playing of instruments, and theory comprise a basic course for all pupils. For those

67

of more than average talent and interest, many additional activities are provided.

Music instruction in the schools not only provides for various forms of performance but also includes many experiences for the listener. Ultimately, the great majority of citizens become listeners or consumers of music and a complete program of music education has the responsibility of giving them contact with some great examples of musical literature and knowledge of the master composers who produce them. The Cleveland five-fold program of music education which brings experiences to pupils in singing, playing, listening, dancing, and creating has become accepted nation-wide and is now officially adopted by the Music Educators National Conference as its "Program of Music Education."

Music in Kindergarten-Primary

In the kindergarten and primary grades an "experience program" is the basis of learning music. Every effort is made to build a love and understanding of music through listening, singing, playing, dancing, and creating. Upon this basis, technical skills can be acquired later quite easily and naturally. In the upper primary there is emphasis on more discriminating listening. The use of music symbols from books and blackboards, as well as ear training, is a foundation for technical instruction.

An investigation of material presented at numerous staff meetings, suggestions to music faculty, and reports to the Superintendent of Schools made by Dr. Morgan as Directing Supervisor of Music of the Cleveland Public Schools reveals that his basic concepts and ideals permeated his work. The material in this chapter has been selected more on a basis of recency than for completeness and should be interpreted by the reader in the light of all that has been presented in this book. The entire first part of the chapter is from "What We Teach," Report of the Superintendent of the Cleveland Public Schools to Board of Education for School Year 1950-51. Dr. Mark Schinnerer, Supt. [Editor]

Content. Singing and listening are closely related in the musical experiences of kindergarten children. For this reason it is essential that the teacher sing frequently for them. In this way young children are helped to form a correct idea of what singing is, before trying to do it themselves. At both kindergarten and first grade levels, seasonal songs and songs related to the interests and activities of the child world are learned. It is here, too, that the building of a repertory of standard folk and patriotic songs begins.

Listening is the foundation of the musical experience. It is the basic tool both for the child's performance and his appreciation. Quiet listening of the audience type is a most important, but too often neglected, activity for little children. The listening experience may come through a radio broadcast, the phonograph, or the teacher's performance.

A feeling for rhythm is a part of both the singing experience and quiet listening. Rhythmic activity gives children opportunity to express this feeling for rhythm in numerous ways. It is essential that they hear a wide variety of compositions played on the piano or phonograph, as well as many rhythmic patterns played on the tom-tom, drum, or other percussion instrument. In the first grades these experiences are often guided by a radio series. At these levels, music and physical education have much in common.

Children like to play their simple songs on the xylophone, glockenspiel (bells), or piano; also on percussion instruments to accompany songs and dances. A valuable playing activity at this level is the rhythm band, which should always be an outgrowth of the child's own musical experience, not a teacher-imposed performance.

Any original musical expression resulting from reaction to fine music, such as a pattern of rhythmic movement, a dance, or a tune to sing or play, constitutes a creative experience for the child.

Three radio series bringing music instruction directly into

69

the classroom are offered under the titles of Rhythmic Activities, Rote Songs by Radio, and Music for Young Listeners. This is the twenty-sixth year for certain of these music-radio educational offerings.

MUSIC IN UPPER ELEMENTARY GRADES

In the upper elementary grades the work outlined previously is to be continued and in addition the reading of music is emphasized. It is reasonable to assume that such emphasis will result in increased appreciation and independence for many children. With the growth of reading power comes the ability to sing more difficult music such as rounds and part songs. The preparation for the educational concerts presented by the Cleveland Orchestra is a part of the regular program for these grades.

All music activities in the elementary schools—listening lessons, vocal music, instrumental music and rhythmic activities—have so much in common that the teaching correlates rather than isolates each of these activities.

Correlation with other subjects offers many natural and effective opportunities. However, the music staff guards against some correlations since they too often force the use of material of little intrinsic worth merely because of a name relationship. To have educational and cultural value, music must preserve its own standards of taste and aesthetic values.

Content. The required course of music for grades four, five, and six includes song literature from the folk art of all countries as well as certain selected songs of the master composers. Every child in these grades has a carefully prepared program of listening and from this repertoire certain numbers are selected for performance by the Cleveland Orchestra in its Little Folks and Young Peoples Educational Concerts. The number of fourth, fifth, and sixth graders who attended these concerts during 1951-52 was 52,340.

A series of radio lessons, entitled "Song Study," is given for upper elementary classes. These weekly lessons present carefully prepared material directly, in the classrooms of certain upper elementary classes.

School choirs are for those of outstanding vocal talent in the upper elementary grades. They consist of the very best voices in the building and their purpose is not only to provide for this outstanding vocal talent but to present within the building a quality of performance which will serve to improve all vocal instruction. Some schools have choirs in the primary grades. In this activity 2,460 children participate.

A broad instrumental program is available for pupils of these grades. Seashore Tests given by radio provide information concerning the accuracy of musical hearing for applicants to these special classes. Orchestras are in many of these schools and at present have 1,666 members. Instrumental classes are available as follows: piano with 1,225 pupils, string instruments with 172 pupils, wind instruments with 88 pupils, and percussion with 15 pupils.

Assembly singing by the whole school, special programs presented for the children of the school, occasional singing by one class for another, and performances by outside artists provide a stimulus that gives vitality and meaning to classroom work.

Music in Junior High School

The arts, since they are distinctively the product of the emotions—an effort to realize an ideal—offer unique opportunities in the junior high school situation. And music, because it presents emotion directly, even to its physical foundations of rhythm and because it is a group activity, is especially valuable in emotional and social development.

The junior high school program attempts to develop love of music as a beautiful and satisfying expression of universal feeling. Experience in music may occur in three ways: by listening to the performance of others, by singing and playing for one's self, and by composing. This love of music, which is accepted as the fundamental purpose of music education, should never be interpreted as keeping the child happy by giving him what he likes, regardless of its musical value. The job of the teacher is to select music within the pupil's immediate range of interest, yet possessing musical value.

Content. Every junior high school has required courses in music for seventh and eighth grade pupils. These courses combine singing and listening as well as some basic theoretic instruction. The work of four semesters is intended to give a general background in music for all pupils of these grades.

The literature of music, from folk song to symphony, is rich in materials which appeal to the junior high pupil. In choosing these, there is enough formal or absolute music to give historic bearings and to satisfy the sensitiveness to form which is often strong at this age. In presenting the works of the older masters, however, the human side is carefully brought out.

VOCAL. The elective vocal groups include mixed chorus, glee clubs, boy choirs, and various ensembles, all presented with the purpose of providing varied opportunity for developing degrees of interest and ability. A total of 1,889 pupils participates in these elective vocal groups.

INSTRUMENTAL. The instrumental program provides a number of activities for boys and girls of talent. Every junior high school has an orchestra and band. The size and quality will vary, but they are of value to the pupil and useful to the school and community. In most of the junior high schools there are instrumental ensembles such as string quartets and clarinet quartets, as well as instrumental classes where players are developed on certain instruments lacking in the major organizations. The enrollment of instrumental activities is 1,915.

LISTENING. The listening program is primarily included in the required music course, but some schools provide an elective course in the ninth grade for those who want to continue their contact with great music. The Cleveland Orchestra presents specially planned educational concerts during both semesters. Preparation for these concerts is provided by scholarly notes available to all teachers and pupils and through recordings enabling all students to become well acquainted with the various masterworks they are to hear.

Music in Senior High School

Hundreds of thousands of Cleveland citizens listen to music each week in churches, theaters, concert halls, and over the radio, and tens of thousands assemble each week to experience the joy of producing vocal and instrumental music. In view of this expressed desire for musical experience, it seems logical that the educational system concern itself with methods of gaining the maximum satisfaction in return for the time and energy expended.

Individuals will differ in need and desire for such training and will vary in ability to profit by a music education program. High school pupils might well be divided into four groups: first, a small group wishing vocational training; second, a much larger proportion wanting to produce music as a form of recreation; third, a large number desiring training in how to listen to the music that constantly surrounds them; and fourth, a very small number without interest or ability in music. It is the third group—the consumers of music—that need development at the high school level. Perhaps this is to be the next great advance in the music program of the Cleveland public schools.

The attitude of pupils toward the subject of music is

rather easily measured by the fact that approximately one-third choose this subject as a part of the school program (music is not required in the senior high school).

Content. All music classes in the senior high school are elective.

INSTRUMENTAL. Instrumental music includes such classes as the orchestra, the band, the various instrumental ensemble groups, and instrumental classes. Among the instrumental ensembles are the string quartets, the wood-wind quintet, and many other combinations that make it possible to carry music making into the home and community. Instrumental classes, as in the junior high school, provide for the development of certain instruments that would otherwise be lacking in the instrumentation of these groups. Here again emphasis is on the quality of the musical literature, on the quality of performance, and upon the development of enthusiasm for hearing and playing music. (Elective—Enrollment 1,259)

LISTENING. The listening program, frequently referred to as Music Appreciation, needs to be more highly developed in secondary schools. While a large number of boys and girls who like to play and sing are provided for in high school classes, there is a still larger group whose interests need to be developed.

THEORY AND HISTORY. In developing musicianship, it is essential that classes be available in the theory of music and the history of music. A few Cleveland high schools offer such classes. (Elective—Enrollment 206)

VOCAL. Every high school, except one technical school, offers a variety of activities in vocal music. These activities include mixed chorus, boys' glee clubs, girls' glee clubs, various ensemble groups such as Madrigal singers, girls' triple trio, and boys' octet. In addition, certain schools offer voice classes where students are developed in the field of solo singing. All of these voice classes have a triple purpose, namely, acquaintance with the best musical literature, appreciation of good musical interpretation, and development of the ability to sing well. (Elective—Enrollment 3,707)

The varying courses in music curriculum are the actual outcome of the different degrees of interest in music evident in the various schools. Most high schools now find it possible to offer a major in music which receives three units of credit and consists of a balanced course including both applied and theoretical music.

For the many whose interest in music is avocational, it is possible to secure two units of credit in music as a minor subject. Naturally there are many whose major interests are in other fields and who yet want some small contact with fine arts and music and therefore elect certain music courses.

DEVELOPING A COMPLETE MUSIC EDUCATION PROGRAM *

Five steps in the music education program:
  A. Philosophy
  B. Objectives
  C. Curriculum
  D. Instruction
  E. Attainment

A. Philosophy
  1. The reality of the unreal
  2. Music making as a craft and as an art
  3. Music for producer and consumer
  4. Music as a vibrant emotional and aesthetic expres-

* It is quite customary for city directors of music to schedule a meeting of all faculty members in their department shortly after the school term opens in the fall, in order to discuss the school program for the term, to integrate new teachers into the system, to establish a unity of purpose, and to set standards for achievement. The outline above, entitled "Developing a Complete Music Education Program," was prepared and used by Dr. Morgan at his opening music faculty meeting held September 18, 1951, and serves here as a summary. [*Editor*]

sion, rather than "cold storage memory and digital dexterity"

5. Seize the moment of excited curiosity for maximum accomplishment
6. The "teachable moment" is not merely a measurement of time in which a child can learn a given fact. The "teachable moment" occurs when certain factors are present; i.e., when a child's interest has been aroused, when he has the incentive to learn, and when he is equipped with tools or skills to pursue the subject in which he is interested
7. Four types of musical experience
    a. Intellectual
    b. Physical
    c. Sensory
    d. Emotional
8. Analysis of musical talent
    a. Personality and leadership
    b. Health and physical energy
    c. Sensory acuteness (eye and ear)
    d. Muscular coordination
    e. Emotional power
    f. Musicality and musical imagination
    g. General intelligence
    h. Interest and will power
B. Objectives
    1. Characteristics of an effective citizen
        a. Objective reasoning
        b. Social responsibility
        c. Effective person to person relationship
        d. Realistic acceptance of self
        e. Discrimination in values
        f. Sense of beauty
        g. Vocational adjustment
        h. Physical competence

    2. Four objectives of the North Central Association of Secondary Schools and Colleges.*

        a. Development and maintenance of high standards of excellence

        b. Continued improvement of the educational program and the effectiveness of instruction through a scientific and professional approach to the solution of educational problems

        c. Establishment of cooperative relationships

        d. Maintenance of effective working situations

    3. Many other studies involving objectives from a previously developed philosophy

C. Curriculum

    1. The Cleveland Five Point Program

    2. Music Educators National Conference outline

    3. The Source Book in Music Education

    4. Basic textbooks

    5. Clarification of the creative experience in music education

D. Instruction

    1. Types of teaching techniques

        a. Research method

        b. Lecture method

        c. Discussion method

        d. Practice or drill method

        e. Demonstration method

        f. Laboratory or experimental method

        g. Project method

        h. Dramatization

        i. Self-directed activity

        j. Question method

        k. Student reports

* Adapted from "The North Central Association Quarterly," July 1950, page 133.

      l. Recitation
        (1) Topical
        (2) Socialized
     m. Visual and aural education
     n. Inductive methods
     o. Deductive methods
     p. Rote method
  2. Lessons Plans
     a. A clear understanding of purpose
     b. Organization and material
     c. Arouse the interest of the children
     d. Clarity and accuracy of understanding
     e. Measurement of attainment
     f. Clarity of assignment
E. Attainment
  1. Testing, grading, and identification of the contribution of music to richer living for the individual and his participation in the musical activities in home, school, church and community

Some General Observations
  1. Unity of purpose but not uniformity of activities
  2. Child centered rather than subject centered
  3. Education is an inner growth of the child rather than a veneer. Operate on the Organismic and Gestalt psychologies.

Thirteen points that guide our Cleveland School Music Program:

  1. The social values secured through music activity
  2. The development of deep and thorough musicianship
  3. The recognition of the importance of the literature of music, just as we consider English literature to be representative of the artistic ideals of English-speaking countries

4. The creative attitude, with its determination to reconstruct the innermost thought of the composer, rather than being content with the outward form of pitch and time

5. The scientific approach to problems in music education, with the intent of finding the most efficient and valuable ways of promoting our educational program

6. Correlation and integration as a way of making music a normal part of sane and beautiful living

7. The integrity of music as a subject, with the thought that music has things to say to the human race that no other art or science can express

8. A belief in the efficacy of principles of education, rather than in the use of specific methods

9. Differentiation with its provision for varying needs and capacities in music

10. The inventive and creative turn of mind which seeks to make available for use in music education all the modern inventions

11. The bringing in of music organizations of the community to act as additions to the faculty of a school

12. A desire to face squarely the values inherent in music education without resorting to false enthusiasm and exploitation

13. Everyone likes some kind of music. The problem is to contact the responsive level of the individual and to develop consciousness of its place in the whole program of musical activity

9

SUPERVISION

AND ADMINISTRATION

"I believe in stressing success rather than emphasizing failure. By that I mean doing everything in my power to bring out the high points of each music teacher, with the thought that they serve as pacemakers for the work of the whole music department. This is opposed to the practice which spends the major portion of its time and thought upon the weak spots, which results in a general leveling off of rather low quality."

R.V.M.

Each town or city tends to develop its own particular organization and policy for supervision and administration, just as individuals differ in personality; but the basic purposes must always remain the same—to improve the teaching of children.

SUPERVISION

Supervision in the educational field has been changing as markedly as any other phase of instruction. Introduced at first as a means of securing instructors with specific training in a given subject, it next expanded to include direction of other teachers not so well prepared in that subject. Following this phase, there came the period when the new conception of principalship placed chief emphasis on supervision of instruction, with much of the administrative work delegated to assistant principals and office clerks. In the past we find that the majority of principals looked upon music, art, and certain so-called special subjects as entirely outside their field of supervisory responsibility. If a question was raised, their shoulders were shrugged and they stated that responsibility for that particular subject rested with some individual called a supervisor. The country-wide shift in this feeling is having far-reaching effects. Today the principal of a school must accept full responsibility for all the instruction that goes on within the classrooms under his administration. This has marked a great forward stride in the teaching of all special subjects. Music and art now usually receive attention equal to that given other subjects.

With this change, the question arises as to just what is the work of the supervisor if the principal takes over supervisory activity in all fields? In the first place, the music supervisor can be only an occasional visitor who cannot possibly follow the work in the classroom as well as a principal who is continually in the building. In the second place, the supervisor cannot know all the many administrative problems of the individual school and therefore a great many problems concerning the special subject must be handled by the principal of the building. The music supervisor can and must be the accepted authority in the field of his subject. His duties thus become more and more that of a "consulting engineer," or an expert adviser, whose opinion is to be valued highly and put into actual practice in so far as it is possible to do so. The supervisor's musicianship and leadership must be such that he is naturally accepted as the final authority on all content problems of his subject.

An important question facing supervision today is that of constantly improving the teaching group while in service. The majority of elementary teachers are somewhat better prepared to teach music today and in most school systems the organization provides for departmentalization on the secondary level, which permits the placing of thoroughly trained music teachers on the school faculty. This question must be faced squarely and considerable attention given to the improvement of instruction.

The Organization and Allotment of the Supervisor's Time. Supervision calls for two distinct types of activity which may well be described by the phrase "the cloister and the crowd." By this I mean that no supervisor, or for that matter any other educator, will be able to preserve a sane and balanced view of his problems unless he definitely reserves time in which he may be alone and undisturbed. On the other hand, it is just as essential that the supervisor be able to mingle freely and easily with other people and help them to understand clearly the program which he offers.

Three divisions of activity are suggested: (1) *the field,* in which the supervisor must carry on inspection, teacher guidance, demonstration lessons, etc., (2) *the office,* where administration and organization problems may be handled and where appointments and conferences may be held, (3) *the time for research and study,* either in the office, if it is possible to work undisturbed, or in some other location where continuous and uninterrupted thought may be given the development of curriculum, selection of materials, and like problems.

It is recognized that an important phase of the supervisor's job is community contacts and time must be allotted for it. These contacts should be kept at a minimum, for it is well known that they constantly crowd and push for attention and can easily cause the supervisor to reach the place where he feels that he is working for everyone else except the school board.

Most of us in supervisory work will devote some such proportion of time to the various activities as follows: 70 per cent in the field, 25 per cent to the office and research, and 5 per cent to community contacts. On the basis of ten half-days in the week, this would mean seven half-days devoted to work in the field and the other day and a half given over to study and office work and some time for P.T.A. speeches and other community contacts. The head supervisor in a large city will probably need to divide his time in a somewhat different manner. Perhaps 40 per cent for the field, 25 per cent for administration, 25 per cent for research, and 10 per cent for community contacts.

It is understood that this time should be carefully budgeted and scheduled. There must be freedom and flexibility for special needs, but without a basic schedule formulated at least tentatively a week in advance, experience has shown that a great deal of time is wasted. Every situation differs, of course, and it remains always with the individual to determine that allotment of time which best suits his personal needs and the needs of the job.

Self-Evaluation. One of the many techniques for analysis and improvement is self-evaluation. An effective supervisor should be able to give an affirmative answer to the following questions:

Do you advise and counsel instead of inspect?

Do you use all available means for contacting teachers without harassment or embarrassment?

Are you thoughtful, considerate, practical, and progressive in your professional requests?

Do you always look at the situation from the teacher's point of view?

Do you demonstrate democratic procedure and encourage interaction in your contacts with teachers?

Is your sincerity apparent and real?

Do you recognize, encourage, and commend creative ability, initiative, and originality in your teachers?

Are your evaluation standards comprehensive and valid?

Are your standards and objectives clearly understood by the teacher?

Are your constructive criticisms based upon sound educational principles?

Do you distribute your visitations to all teachers within a reasonable period?

Do you encourage and accept new ideas and adjust or replace previous ones?

Are you not only willing but eager to spend time helping individual teachers?

Are you continually aware of individual differences in teachers?

Are your suggestions constructive and kindly given?

Are your relationships with teachers and other personnel congenial and relaxed?

Do you often show enthusiasm over a teacher's work?

Do you always have something of value to offer when you visit?

Do you have a sense of humor and does it show?

In addition to the supervisory responsibilities discussed, there is a certain amount of administrative work which falls to the lot of chief supervisors. In small systems, the administrative phase may be very light, but in larger cities the administrative work of the musical director or chief supervisor becomes a rather heavy duty.

ADMINISTRATIVE PROBLEMS IN MUSIC DEPARTMENTS

Administration in the best sense combines organization and management. A music department must be properly organized or its functioning will not and cannot be efficient and effective. Good management is needed for, without that, there is no power to operate the machine. An automobile is an example of unique organization of mechanical principles, but the performance of this potentially perfect organization depends to an astonishing degree upon the ability and purpose of the driver who manages it. It should be clear, then, that both organization and management are essential in the administration of a music department.

Administrative duties are, to some extent, placed upon every member of a school system. Each teacher must organize and manage his classroom and is usually assigned additional administrative duties by the principal's office. Principals and superintendents are primarily charged with administration, although modern educational thought insists that they accept an equal responsibility for supervision of instruction. There are six major administration areas:

1. *Personnel.* In larger cities, the selection of music teachers is handled by a personnel bureau, or some such office, with varying degrees of participation by the head of the music department. In some cases, the music head is responsible for the preparation and grading of applicants' examinations, while in others he is charged with the responsibility of nominating two or three candidates, with final selection being made by the administration. In any case, the following four points are, in my opinion, the basis for choice: (1) musicianship, (2) educational preparation, (3) classroom teaching ability, and (4) personal qualities.

It should be obvious that musicianship is one of the basic

85

qualifications, yet far too many prospective teachers have been content with too limited equipment. Musicianship should include performing ability, a strong background of music history, a broad historical understanding, and the ability to bring all this equipment to bear upon the study and presentation of any musical problem in the classroom. It is my personal opinion that every music instructor should develop unusual performing ability in voice or upon some instrument. Unless the individual has had first-hand experience in artistic production, it is difficult for him to understand what artistry means and to develop it in pupils. Only the rare person can secure artistic results from others without himself being able to perform in more than ordinary fashion.

Interpretation of any fine piece of work hinges partly upon a thorough knowledge of historical background. This does not refer to the chronological dates and names, but rather to that deeper sense of historical background which creates an understanding of the development of musical forms and the artistic and aesthetic purpose of the various musical periods. Theoretical background is an obvious need, as is also ear training, sight singing, and harmony. In the final analysis, the musicianship of the teacher will condition the development of artistic performance in all music classes.

Educational courses are essential, but such courses should be held to a practical minimum. There is a tendency to overload a teacher with too many traditional education courses at the expense of developing scholarship and musical ability. Methods courses, as such, should likewise be held to the minimum, with the exception of practice teaching, which does offer great help to the teacher in training.

Classroom teaching ability is essential. It is not enough to *know*, but a teacher must be able also to communicate both his enthusiasm and his knowledge.

Personal qualities include a great number of points such

as the individual's interest in music and interest in children. The teacher who is not an enthusiastic follower of musical activities cannot transmit the contagion of musical enthusiasm to his pupils. In the same manner, a teacher who is not really interested in a child's development cannot possibly convince boys and girls that he is trying to serve them.

Social relationships are important because a teacher must be able to work smoothly with other members of the faculty and administration. Maximum development of a musical program depends on the cooperation and good wishes of all other members of the faculty. An individual cannot fight disinterest or antagonism in developing a school activity.

The need for health is obvious. After all, any vital musical performance calls for the expenditure of tremendous energy. Analysis of an excellent performance will convince anyone that sheer vitality and energy play a tremendous part in performance and teaching.

It is possible to go on with many other items such as initiative, good judgment, acceptance of responsibility—all items that come under the general heading of "personal qualities" which are so important in the selection of a teacher.

After a teacher has entered a system, administration must accept responsibility for helping to create a situation under which the teacher may grow and develop all possible power and ability. To a certain extent, the development of an individual depends upon the opportunity he has for self-direction and acceptance of responsibilities. Therefore, administration of teachers in service should be pointed toward setting up all possible situations in which the individual will have maximum *opportunity* to grow. All teachers must participate in developing curriculum, choosing materials, and organizing courses, if they are to bring to their classroom work the complete understanding of the purpose of such courses. Every effort should be made to recognize any success attained by individual teachers. It is important that that success be made known to the whole school and to other schools. This serves as one of the most powerful rewards for exceptional work and also immediately sets standards which influence instruction in other schools. After all, a successful music program depends primarily upon the teacher in the classroom, and so it is essential for administration to use every possible way of developing the power and ability of each individual in the schools.

Certification is usually a state responsibility and need not be discussed here, except to say that there is need for more uniformity among various states.

Another question in regard to personnel arises in determining how many and what types of music teachers are needed for any given school system. Teacher-pupil ratio determines the total number of teachers for a system. The board of education, superintendent, and principal all pass judgment upon the percentage of teachers to be allotted to the various subjects. Pupil interest and community approval are powerful factors in this determination. Balance must be preserved in distribution of faculty among subjects, and yet an exceptionally strong interest will always result in a larger number of teachers for any given department. Teacher assignments for required music classes are a constant factor based upon enrollment and class size, but, with elective classes, the number of faculty usually increases as interest grows and causes more students to elect an activity. In a school where tremendous enthusiasm for music has been developed, faculty additions are almost forced upon administration through the resultant pupil demand and community pressure.

2. *Curriculum.* It is possible for the large city to present a curriculum that will preserve quality of instruction and yet provide for a freedom that is essential if proper adjustments are to be made to community differences, school purposes, and instructors' abilities. This may be secured by

determining the real purpose of teaching music and developing the basic principles of music education, and not placing reliance upon specific methods and techniques. Democracy certainly operates here, and should result in the growth of thinking power on the part of each member of the faculty, evidenced in increased initiative and interest. If the true meaning of curriculum is the orderly sequence of successful and significant experiences, then every teacher must have freedom to discover the particular experiences that meet the needs of his specific groups.

3. *Budget.* A school system receives a definite income each year. A superintendent and board of education will attempt to make a fair allotment to each subject field. Demonstrated need for more money usually receives a sympathetic hearing and an effort is made to readjust in apportionment of the budget.

It is necessary to keep in mind, though, the definite limitations in the matter of money. A tax rate provides a specific amount of money and even the most willing board of education cannot add to that money. Frequently the music department, however, can, through its development of community interest, help the board of education to gain more adequate support for its program through increased levies.

Having determined the exact amount of money available for the music program of a given system, the question immediately arises as to how to distribute this money among the various schools and levels of instruction. It would seem obvious that an elementary school needs less than a senior high school because of the increased expense of musical material and the added musical equipment. Then again, in the senior high school, a year's supply of choral music does not cost as much as the music needed for a large band and orchestra. Schools vary in size and these questions immediately come to mind: Shall we apportion money on a per pupil basis, or upon the evidence of musical activity in the school, or upon the different economic situations found among the families of different school districts? Of course, all these factors should be considered in distributing the available money.

In organizing a budget, the board of education divides it into various headings, under which different types of expenditures are placed. In many systems, the following headings are used for actual operating expenses: (1) instructional salaries, (2) textbooks, (3) supplies, (4) equipment, (5) housing, (6) maintenance. In addition, of course, every board has to provide for debt retirement, for custodial salaries, and for many other things not related to music.

INSTRUCTIONAL SALARIES are almost entirely a problem outside music department administration. There is usually a schedule which provides for salaries of all teachers, without reference to subject taught.

TEXTBOOKS are usually a problem in which the music department has to determine the basic books to be used, advisedly by committee action, and the number of books that should be available to each classroom. The problem of buying the books remains entirely in the hands of the school administration offices.

SUPPLIES, as a budget heading, usually includes all octavo, sheet, band, and orchestra music; also phonograph recordings and such printed forms and envelopes and music repair material as are on the approved list. As musical organizations grow, this budget for supplies must be increased enormously in order to prevent starvation of the musical needs of the various classes. The budget needs to be determined every year and allotted among the various activities. It usually is difficult to get enough money for this item, but it devolves upon the music department to use whatever money is available to the very best advantage.

EQUIPMENT includes pianos, band and orchestral instruments, music stands, phonographs, radios, and all other material which is considered reasonably permanent. It is possible to set up the total amount of money needed to equip your schools properly and then, in conference with administrative officials, determine how much of that amount could be set aside for each year. Upon this would rest the determination of whether the equipment program will be a five-year program, an eight-year program, or a ten-year program. Buying at random from year to year is inexcusable even for the individual school. A program must be carefully studied and developed, so that each allotment of budget money can be spent according to a well-thought-out and approved plan.

HOUSING includes any special construction within the rooms, such as instrumental storage, cabinets for music, soundproofing of rooms, risers, etc. Usually, a specified amount is set aside for all items under this heading of housing, and the music department can list only such projects as they think are needed. They are then taken up in order and at a rate of progress dictated by the money available.

MAINTENANCE deserves more attention than it is usually given. A certain amount of the budget must be set aside to maintain the usefulness of the equipment present in the various schools. Pianos must be tuned; band and orchestra instruments must be inspected and repaired; phonographs and radios are many times criminally neglected and mean a large loss that might have been avoided if proper inspection and maintenance had been carried on. So by all means be sure that there is adequate provision for the maintenance of all equipment.

4. *New Equipment, Records, and Services.* Specifications for new equipment are essential, but call for an extended discourse devoted entirely to this topic. Perhaps it is sufficient here to stress the importance of having a workable

record of all school and board-owned instruments which will show valuation, date of purchase, identification marks, cost of maintenance, etc. Many other types of records will need to be kept so that a department will have an accurate picture of its problems—past, present, and future.

The music department also serves as a service department and, in one sense, the supervisor's office is to be measured by the degree of assistance it offers the classroom teacher in carrying out the daily work in the school room. There are many other services which the office can and should offer to the teacher, to the administration, and to the community at large, which will bring about greater respect for and understanding of the music program in the schools.

5. *Unification of School Policy.* The music department is only one of many subject divisions. It has a share in the development of the whole child and, because of this, must discover a way of cooperation that links its purposes with all others in developing a complete and happy child. Sometimes it seems as if the music department merely rents space in a school building to carry on instruction totally unrelated to all other activities in the building. Instead, we must remember that the primary purpose is to educate the child and music is but one of the pathways to this goal.

6. *Public Relations.* The neighborly interest of the small city creates natural interests in the school and those who teach in the schools. In larger cities such personal interest is practically impossible, though the sum total of relationships of the entire teaching force does have a community effect. Public approval determines the kind of school system in which you teach. This approval is easily lost if mistakes are made. Education can lead but only slightly ahead of the understanding and consent of the community. In the end, confidence and interest won through intelligent public relations are the determining factors in the development of a school program.

GUIDANCE

"Power and extended ability can come only through slow, solid growth and patient waiting for recognition."

R.V.M.

The American public school system has been increasingly concerned with the need for a guidance program. When guidance was first brought into the schools, it was thought of simply as a way of offering information concerning the numbers employed in various fields and the monetary reward that could be expected. This was stressed in order that students might have adequate information about ways of making a living, the necessary qualifications for fitting into the various types of work, and the program of school training needed to prepare for this life's work.

Since the introduction of guidance, a new concept of its function has been developed which looks toward the guidance of the individual as a whole and seeks to help him become an acceptable and contributing person in a democratic society. This has led to the use of the term "counselor," in preference to "guidance official."

Counseling of students automatically falls into three major categories—personal, academic, and vocational; but it is

93

not wise to try to isolate any one category because various aspects of each are overlapping and should be integrated. Among the chief aims in this area are those of assisting the student in an acceptance of himself, with a realization of his limitations as well as his abilities; helping him to realize the advantages of desirable behavior; and encouraging the establishment of goals which will give him direction for progress.

It is important for counselors to keep certain basic principles in mind. Local situations, such as traditions, opportunities, and financial status, should enter into the consideration. As soon as a readiness for guidance has been established with the student, he can be helped to see himself in relation to the general as well as the specific aspects of the situation. By encouraging the student to make suggestions for possible solutions and to participate in the development of plans, his self-respect can be retained and stimulated. Choices then can be built, adapted, or replaced without complete destruction of previous concepts. Factors which will promote effective and happy conditions immediately will need consideration along with those for future success.

Methods of procedure should be based upon educational research, the demands of a democracy, a sound philosophy, and a practical use of psychological principles. If all counseling can be based upon complete understanding and a sincere desire to face a situation or problem and *do something constructive about it,* the pupil will soon learn about himself and become progressively independent.

The Guidance Specialist in Music. A great number of secondary schools have some individual on their staffs who has charge of the responsibility of being a guidance counselor for the student body. It seems essential to have someone give at least a large share of his attention to this important problem; but it is immediately obvious that no one individual can be completely equipped to offer expert advice in all fields. Thus every general counselor should find it possible to confer with some individual who can be rated as a specialist in the field of music.

The contribution of the guidance specialist in music would be directed into three channels: (1) establishing a technique for analyzing the capacities of the individual student, (2) formulating policies which would determine whether the student should be directed into vocational or avocational interests in music, and (3) presenting to the student a clear picture of the various divisions in the field of music, together with the possible chance of placement and the normal expectation of financial reward. Because many printed references are available which deal with the third point, only the first two points are considered here.

ANALYSIS OF CAPACITIES

In determining the capacity of the individual, it would be wise to indicate first the types of qualifications that are needed for success. My own listing of these items are (1) sensory keenness, (2) motor ability, (3) emotional capacity, (4) musicality, (5) will power and interest, and (6) general intelligence. It is recognized that there are other attributes which are helpful, such as personality, appearance, etc.

In the field of sensory measurement, we have some rather accurate testing material. We can know, for instance, just how keen the ear is in the matter of pitch and how discriminating it is in the matter of tone quality; we can discover how well an individual is able to retain pitch patterns—all this is basic to musical development. Of course sensory equipment is only one of a number of facets of musical capacity; and while a definite weakness in this field would raise a serious question concerning the advisability of a student attempting to make music a vocation, it is important to remember that the mere possession of high marks in sensory tests does not in any way present a complete picture of talent. It is perfectly possible for a boy or girl possessing a very keen ear to be very weak in musical development. Judgment, or accurate measurement, in any of these categories is only one item which must be included in the list which makes up the total upon which our evaluation of the student must rest, rather than upon the level of ability shown in any specific category.

A demonstration of motor ability has been frequently mistaken for musical talent. In other words, the young person who, through sheer motor dexterity, can play scales and arpeggios at phenomenal speeds is apt to be thought of as having unusual musical talent; whereas it may be that he can never be successful musically, in spite of a remarkable muscular ability to master problems of technique upon an instrument. Here, again, this is only one phase that must be considered with all the others, in order to reach a final judgment.

Measurement of emotional power seems to be elusive, but we can arrive at some reasonably accurate judgments in the matter from competent teachers acquainted with the student. Emotional power must show itself; first, in the capacity to feel in the musical medium, and then in that power of expressing itself through music. We find numbers of students who are quite strongly affected emotionally by a musical experience; but, for one reason or another, they find it almost impossible to release that emotional drive into musical performance. This ability, in my judgment, is one of the essentials in determining musical talent.

By the term musicality is meant that innate gift in dealing with musical materials. Perhaps it can best be expressed by a parallel example in the field of mathematics. We are all aware of the differences that exist among our various friends. Some struggle desperately to keep a check book in balance; others find it difficult to keep a bridge score properly; then again, someone we know seems to have an almost uncanny sense in solving mathematical problems and making figures behave. It is this same capacity in the field of music that I term "musicality." It amounts to almost an intuition—an almost unconscious sensing of what is right in music. Here again, we seem to have no particular measuring stick, but fairly accurate judgments can be afforded by competent teachers acquainted with the student.

Only infrequently is will power rated as one of the essentials for success. Interest, yes; everyone recognizes that interest in the subject is really essential for development of power and ability; but I would like to call your attention to the term "will power." I have seen so many otherwise gifted students fade from the musical picture because their will power was not strong enough to impose the self-discipline and continuous application that is one of the essentials for success.

Vocational and Avocational Interests

There should be a real distinction between the equipment demanded for a student expecting to enter music as a vocation, and that of the student who only desires music education for the preparation of avocational activity or a hobby. There are great numbers of our high school boys and girls who can well be encouraged to carry on the study of music, with the thought that it will make a significant contribution to the leisure time part of their lives. But there are very definite limitations upon the opportunities in the field of professional music, and it seems to me that only those with superlative talent should be given encouragement to enter this field. At times I am even tempted to use a negative approach to this problem of guidance for vocational music; that is, to tell students that if they can possibly keep away from music as a vocation, to do so. It seems to me that a student should have an all-consuming desire to live in music before he is ready to face the years of hard work, discouragements and rebuffs that will surely confront him in professional life.

Composers Are Needed. A number of years ago, in the days of silent pictures, the orchestra director of a theater assembled such music as he thought fitting and performed it as an accompaniment to the picture. With the advent of sound pictures, the musical setting still remained largely an editing process in the field of musical materials but was, of course, more carefully handled.

There is a strong and growing demand for original scores in connection with motion pictures, radio, and television. This extends all the way from major symphonic scores, through background music, to singing commercials. There are definite indications that this stimulus is leading to a renaissance in composition. Every great sweep of the development of musical form and its vitality in expression has been because of the interest aroused through some particular medium. It may be the fascination of vocal counterpoint; it may be the organizing of dance forms into a suite. There is evidence that scores written especially for sound pictures have real concert value.

Young composers who are familiar with the needs and abilities of school music groups, possibly due to recency of membership in such groups, would do well to direct some of their talent in composition toward serving this ever-present market for suitable materials.

Conductors Needed for Civic Groups. The need for skilled conductors of civic music organizations is encountered in all areas of musical performance, both choral and instrumental; bands, orchestras, choirs, and opera groups.

Summer bands, often organized in connection with civic recreational programs, present a splendid opportunity for conductors who are alert to the unique requirements of this type of musical activity.

Many medium-sized cities have players who could form a

creditable civic orchestra with proper and energetic promotion. In some instances players have been drawn from several neighboring towns. The existence of such civic orchestras usually depends upon the availability of suitable conductors.

Throughout all the states of our nation there is a growing interest in civic choral groups and, in the judgment of many people, the only deterrent in this field is an amazing lack of skilled choral conductors—conductors who possess personality, conducting power, knowledge of voice and fundamental musicianship. Thousands of young people leave schools every year with an inclination towards choral singing, but without the stimulus of fine adult organizations to attract them as members. This is primarily a problem of leadership and must be a challenge to some of those who graduate from our great music schools and conservatories.

Groups desiring to rehearse and produce opera are springing up all over our country. These productions are a delight to those who perform as well as to those who listen but require adequate direction.

Another movement of great power is that of the artistic amateur who needs continued teaching. How many private teachers realize their responsibility for organizing and coaching ensembles among their students? These students must have some form of outlet and experience, or their training seems entirely futile to them and, to a large extent, it will probably be just that.

The whole concept of guidance is a challenge to music educators for a re-dedication to increased efforts in understanding and presenting music; a re-dedication of the integrity and ideals which have imbued us during the years of training; and a re-dedication to that loyalty to music and its great mission to mankind which will illumine and make meaningful music as a chosen life work.

11
COMMUNITY ACTIVITIES
AND RELATIONSHIPS

*"The people of our country sense values in
the fine arts although they frequently are unable to give any specific reason for such reaction. It is this intangible but real understanding
of music's power that gives the American public
the desire to secure for the coming generation
the beauty and enrichment of life which so
many of them have been unable to find."*

R.V.M.

Music education in our schools today is primarily
concerned with making it possible for great numbers of our
citizens to become musical amateurs. There is no thought
of training great numbers in a vocational sense, nor of over-
crowding the professional field of music making. It is rather
the desire of the schools to create a great body of people
who are vitally interested in making music of their own,
with no expectation of any return save that of the happiness
that comes through the creation or recreation of something
beautiful. True enough, this program will make it possible
for many more people to secure a more understanding and

happier experience in listening to those whose business it is to perform in a musical way.

Many things indicate that America, as a national community, is gaining a truer conception of the real life values. We begin to see that we have been over-concerned with the making of *things*, with the thought that they would constitute satisfaction in our living. We know, of course, that we must find ways of earning a living; but we have begun to understand that the thing of chief importance is how to live this life we support. Education is coming more and more to the belief that the value of our civilization is not measured in things that man can be taught to produce, but by the manner of man produced.

The field of the fine arts was nourished, for many centuries, by the wealthy nobility of the different nations, and only certain elemental phases of folk dancing and folk singing were available to the common man. The democracy of America holds that the great things of beauty should be in the possession of every man, no matter what his economic or social standing in the community. To this end, America has placed music in the educational curriculum of our public school system and has consistently supported every attempt to expand the lives of all our children by sensitizing their souls to the great beauty that resides in all the fine arts.

The High School Musician Inspects the Music in the Community

A large number of boys and girls are very active in the music programs of our senior high schools. Because of this we are confronted with the problem of helping them to use this ability after graduation. While we hold that the experience of music in the high school is in itself of sufficient value to justify a strong curriculum in this subject, nevertheless full fruition of this work depends upon opportunities for continuing musical activity when school is over.

101

The boys and girls actively engaged in music from an avocational standpoint form an astonishingly large group. In the nation as a whole they approximate one-third of the total high school enrollment. We are naturally interested in knowing what proportion of these young people continue the musical interest shown at high school age in their after lives, and in discovering what various attractions draw them to the large number of adult community music groups.

We may gain some information on the problem of student interest in adult activities by informing ourselves of their community and home music contacts while they are still students of the school. It is evident, in many cases, that social leanings determine membership in the majority of cases. Students join an organization as a rule because of a personal friendship with those who are already members of the group. Guidance does not seem to carry us far in placing these pupils in the different organizations. This perhaps is a wise outcome and, after all, we have trained these people not to serve music but to use music to secure the richest possible leisure time and social relationships. Therefore, in the majority of cases, it seems much the better course to permit the students to make their own normal musical relationships outside of the school, thus relieving them of that hovering type of guidance which seems to command the activities of every individual. In other words, it would seem that the student should have free choice in his after-school music relationships, rather than be forced to submit to a regimentation conceived by some individual or small group as best for all people concerned. Democracy does not operate in this fashion.

What responsibility then does the high school have to music graduates? Obviously the music department should give the most complete information possible concerning all phases of music activity in the community and the ways in which contacts may be made with these various organizations. We may go a step beyond that and establish a card catalog of all music graduates, which in turn can be made available to the directors and officers of the various community music groups. They in turn may then extend invitations to our graduates, which may or may not be accepted.

It might be well to consider some of the various musical activities of the community in which the graduate may find pleasurable membership.

1. In every city there are well-known amateur organizations whose strength may depend upon tradition and organization, or may center about the personality of the leader. In larger cities there are, of course, great numbers of these vocal and instrumental groups. Not long ago the Singers' Club, one of Cleveland's outstanding male choruses, invited several of the glee clubs of high school boys to their rehearsal room for an evening of singing and good-fellowship. This seemed valuable from the standpoint of both groups. The great majority of members recruited, however, are secured through the personal contact of members with singers graduated from the city's schools.

2. There are a large number of nationality vocal and instrumental groups in Cleveland. In the majority of cases the groups have existed over a great many years and are highly organized and possess great strength. In the larger cities these nationality music groups are well worth support by the schools.

3. The social settlements offer opportunities for continuing the music activity of high school graduates in less economically favored sections of a city. Strong programs of choral and instrumental music can be organized in these districts, where music would otherwise be a rare experience.

4. A large number of lodges and clubs sponsor musical or-

ganizations for both younger and older musicians, many of them achieving musical results of high order.

5. In some communities industrial and commercial firms have developed very active musical programs. Many cases are known where outstanding performers desired by these business organizations have been given positions on the regular payroll in order that their talent might be available in the employee musical unit.

6. The adult education movement has brought about a strong development of the evening schools and community centers, where an ever-increasing program of musical activities may be carried forward.

7. Some high schools have emphasized alumni musical organizations. If such groups come into being in a spontaneous and natural way, a great service is being rendered. But if this is only an attempt to continue regimentation, largely for the purpose of spreading the influence and prestige of either a music teacher or a high school, the activity should be questioned rather severely. This much is surely obvious, that alumni organizations can never hope to cover all the individuals with musical interest and they, therefore, assume a place as one unit in a large collection of musical activities in the community.

8. Some mention should be made of musical organizations in the home and neighborhood. They exist in a surprising number, but because there is no attendant publicity or public performances, the value and joy present in these spontaneous units is sometimes overlooked. Naturally, the churches serve as a base for a great deal of choral music and a number of them in Cleveland have flourishing instrumental groups. One question raised occasionally concerns the value of offering so much opportunity for choral music in the high schools when the graduates seem to take so little interest in the music of the church.

It would seem that this inquiry is based upon insufficient information. For instance, a survey made several years ago, covering approximately twenty-five per cent of the Protestant churches in Cleveland, discovered that the membership of the choirs numbered approximately 4000 and that the age groups in these church choirs were distributed in such a way that sixty per cent of the membership fell between the ages of sixteen and twenty-five. These figures, indicating that sixty per cent of our choirs are young people just out of school, would lead us to raise the question: What has happened to the support that should be given by the older people to the music program of the church?

Another point in connection with church music is of real importance. In every city of the United States, choral music is being presented as a part of worship every Sunday in the year. In addition to that, hundreds of thousands of men and women are participating in singing hymns each Sunday. This would seem to be a remarkable activity in the choral field and needs much more attention than as yet has been given it.

Music Education's Responsibility to the Church Choir. American government is built upon the separation of church and state, which of course involves separation of churches and public schools. Nevertheless, I feel that graduates of public school vocal groups could well be urged to transfer their interest and ability to the choir of the church of their own denomination.

Volunteer church choirs with excellent conductors have small trouble in maintaining a large membership of better than average ability. I am convinced that practically all of the troubles of the church choir are due primarily to the weakness of the conductor. Of course, I can turn right around and in perfect truth say that the weakness of the public school chorus is almost entirely a reflection of weakness of the conductor or teacher. This weakness may be lack of personality, lack of musicianship, or laziness in seeking out worth-while material, inability to organize and a host of other causes that any reader could easily list.

One thing that provides an easy transition from school choir to church choir is the fact that much fine choral music is sacred, and that the leading choruses in schools have quite an unusual acquaintance with sacred music and with the traditions of performance of the various schools such as Palestrina and his group, the modern Russian, and the modern English groups.

I believe every individual has a strong urge towards some religious expression and I believe that there is nothing more fitting than the use of one's best talent in the service of that religion. Therefore it would seem a proper thing for school music people to take a decided interest in the development and conducting of church music, particularly as it concerns the church choir.

The assuming of this work presupposes an interest in church music and that the fundamental training of a school music teacher provides many of the basic needs for handling church music. Such an individual must bring a sincere desire to aid others in the worship of God, and there must also be present the unique ability to handle the volunteer service of adults. There must be a strong desire to make an exhaustive search for good music that carries a message.

It does not seem to me inconsistent to receive a salary for this work, particularly as in most cases the cost of preparation for such work was extremely high. I do feel strongly that salaries asked should be quite consistent with the financial strength of the church organization and never cause that organization to assume such a heavy burden that financial worry detracts from enjoyment of musical results.

The basic ideas expressed concerning the responsibility of

music educators to the church choir can be applied equally as well to all types of community music activities and organizations.

Summary. In summation, the following observations may be made. High school students become active in music because music contributes something of richness to their lives. Upon graduation they should retain freedom of choice in making contacts with musical groups in the community. With this freedom, however, there remains the obligation of the high school to offer some guidance program which will acquaint music students with all of the opportunities available in their community and furnish, in so far as is possible, means of contact with these various music groups.

As the high school musician inspects the music of his community, he becomes aware of a great number of choruses and instrumental groups busily engaged in providing musical pleasure and he becomes intelligent in his choice of affiliation. This after all is the greatest thing a school can do for an individual, give him clear and accurate information and an attitude that will cause him to choose that which is best for himself and the social life of the community.

MUSIC AND THE TAXPAYER

Our educational program is subject to expansion and contraction according to the economic situation of the country as a whole, which directly affects the community. In times of prosperity the American people are inclined to consider favorably additional tax expense for almost any activity in the schools that has a determined and sincere backing. However, during times of stress there is always an attempt to weigh objectives and values of all activities in the school program, with a view of curtailing those areas which might seem to make the least contribution to the ultimate educational goal.

More than a century of music in our schools has been

completed. In recent years the music program has expanded at a rapid rate and, of course, costs have risen. This brings up the question, "Just how much musical education should be provided by the American taxpayer for the children in our schools?"

Let us keep in mind the fact that passive acceptance has been given the program in times of prosperity, but we should know specifically what contribution to American education music educators can point to as the result of their music teaching.

Our conception of educational purposes are constantly changing and today we think in terms of providing the individual with means for enrichment of his life as well as provision for the support of that life. Many have attempted to build a short but inclusive list of educational objectives acceptable to the taxpayer as well as to the profession. For our purpose here, let us accept the four ultimate objectives in education as set up by the North Central Association of Secondary Schools and Colleges: namely, (1) Health, (2) Social Relationships, (3) Right Use of Leisure Time, and (4) Vocational (including explorational activities).

Health. Undoubtedly music contributes to both mental and physical health. There is also the possibility of music becoming vocational preparation. The contributions to these two objectives, however, is not quite so obvious as it is in the case of social relationships and the right use of leisure time. For that reason, the following discussion will be confined to showing how music justifies the spending of tax money and how music contributes to these two particular objectives in education.

Social Values. Music education possesses social value and art value. The combination is practical and wholesome. There is much argument as to which value is to be placed first. Everyone is familiar with teachers who place all emphasis on the social side, expressing their ideas through community singing and a general hullabaloo of noisy good-fellowship. We also know musicians who worship the art of music with such blind adoration that they ignore the human side, forgetting that all art serves its highest purpose only so far as it contributes to enrichment of life for man.

A music program emphasizing the social objective exclusively will soon fail through sheer inertia, because the power plant of artistic stimulation is missing. In other words, the social objective is properly served only when there is steady growth in the comprehension and love of the art.

Social life in the home centers around small music groups. The possibility of thousands of graduates forming small ensembles for the enrichment of their own home life presents a clear cut challenge to music teachers sincerely interested in attaining a full realization of the social relationships objective. Europe has had a strong development of this activity for years. Its practice in America would have a profound effect upon the social life of the community and nation. Perhaps it isn't too wishful to think of finding homes in every neighborhood in which groups are gathering for the purpose of singing interesting part songs or playing music by the masters arranged for small ensembles of string and woodwind instruments.

Leisure Time. Music holds a high place among the activities useful for proper development of the leisure time objective. Even the careless performance of light music may have some small value, and concentration upon fine compositions may repay the individual enormously in terms of spiritual growth and aesthetic power. Contact with beauty in any form makes life richer for the individual.

It may seem trite to say that everything at present points toward increased leisure time for a large proportion of the American population, but it is nevertheless a serious problem which every community must face. Contentment is never secured through possession of things, but only through a realization of growth in personality, power and worth to the world, or that particular part of it with which one comes in contact. Music may well be one of the bulwarks of defense against disintegration of the idle individual. So long as work was a heavy taskmaster the problem was not crucial, but with a great deal of leisure some constructive activity must be available to the individual in every community if the very fiber of character is not to weaken. Music is one of the best activities for the healthy, sane use of free time.

It is easy to believe that the American people will wholeheartedly support the use of tax money for a music program which contributes so strongly to education when they clearly realize its purposes and attainments. They must be convinced that the teachers know what they are about and that the machinery of the school functions in a way that will permit the educator to reach these objectives. The people of our country sense value in the fine arts, even though they are frequently unable to give any specific reason for such a reaction. It is this intangible understanding of music's power that gives the American public the desire to secure for the coming generation the beauty and enrichment of life which so many of them have been unable to find.

When economic problems arise which take away from us the material things we once possessed, we realize to a greater extent the eternal happiness that comes from having spiritual and aesthetic resources within one's self that no man can take away. As I say to the children in our schools, we want each individual so developed in mind and spirit that he can find within himself the possibility of creating his own happiness. My words to the children are sometimes these: "Can you knock on your own forehead and find anyone at home with whom you can enjoy yourself?" If this has been accomplished, the child will become a worthy member not only of his locale, but of the world community.

12 OVERVIEW

"The power music has exerted in the world is evidenced by its prominent position in the emotional life of man.

"A world without music would be unthinkable, for we have come to realize that full, rich living demands contact with the fine arts, something which is beautiful and nourishes the soul."

R.V.M.

A brief summary or overview of the material in this book is condensed into the following outline which was prepared by Dr. Morgan for use originally at a music faculty meeting. While it is directed chiefly toward the elementary grade level, the thinking behind it is equally applicable to the secondary level. [*Editor*]

PART I—SOME PHILOSOPHIES OF MUSIC EDUCATION

1. Intelligence, emotion, and aesthetics in art education
2. Skills, knowledges, and appreciations
3. Music making as a craft and as an art
4. The creative attitude in teaching

5. Dominance of emotional training over mental training in music education
6. Discussion of the logical versus psychological approach to music instruction
7. Social and art values in music education
8. What is good music? (quality of materials)
9. Analysis of musical talent
10. The need for fine leadership
11. The need for clear understanding of and feeling response to what is good musical expression

(*Can you put your own philosophy into words?*)

PART II—Basic Needs in Music Education

1. Clear understanding of objectives, including such specific topics as:
   a. A strong emotional response to music
   b. A sense of freedom and exaltation after musical experience
   c. A pleasure and pride in ability to perform
   d. An interest in the construction of music
   e. Willingness to contribute talent for the enjoyment of others
2. Desirable attributes of the principal
   a. Genuine interest in music
   b. Willingness to feel responsibility for:
      (1) Teaching procedures
      (2) Schedule problems
      (3) Material
      (4) Programs—both for motivation and for their effect upon school and community
   c. The use of the *best* talent among the teachers
      There is no advantage in departmental organization if the teachers are not outstanding

112

3. The teacher must have some very definite qualifications. This is a suggestive list:
   a. Emotional power
   b. Discrimination
   c. Musical intelligence
   d. Accurate ear
   e. Knowledge of what good tone really is
   f. Good leadership
   g. Something of showmanship
   h. Ability to throw out the non-essential material and concentrate only on worth-while things
   i. Ability to sing and play piano in a *musical way*
   j. A real hunger for contact with good music

4. Vocal study is definitely a laboratory subject; but frequently help comes when definite attention is drawn to the following:
   a. Tone quality
   b. Tone color
   c. Pitch
   d. Dynamics
   e. Articulation
   f. Enunciation
   g. Pronunciation
   h. Breath control
   i. Flexibility
   j. Vocal drills
   k. Chord drills

5. The accompaniment should always live up to its name and never assume leadership. Accompaniments are usually much too heavy and unmusical.

6. Rhythm is extremely important:
   a. Muscular response, pendulum swing, etc.
   b. Basis of all comprehension of musical form
   c. Lack of good rhythm effectively prevents any worth-while musical experience
   d. There must be muscular activity and ear training in connection with rhythm. It applies through action, singing, listening, playing, rhythm orchestra, etc.

113

7. Pitch—accuracy of ear coupled with accuracy of tone production

8. Programs
   a. Always use music of real quality
   b. Do not overlook showmanship
   c. Problems of program building
   d. Handling of groups, etc.

9. Supervision
   a. Includes
      (1) Inspection and evaluation
      (2) Research, to be used in future planning
      (3) Teacher Training and Guidance
   b. Is
      (1) Philosophic
      (2) Cooperative
      (3) Creative
      (4) Scientific
      (5) Effective

PART III—Specific Problems

1. Tone. Instruction pointed toward preservation of voice rather than development of solo voice.

2. Appreciation. The chief objective of music education is appreciation—whether listening, singing or playing. Some music is wonderfully fitted for children to hear though its difficulty is such as to prevent performance by children. This material forms the reservoir from which listening lessons are organized.

   Children's Concerts are "live exhibits"—a laboratory for perfect presentation of a rich artistic experience. Preparation is essential as is "follow-up."

   Appreciation is chiefly concerned with right attitudes and reactions to emotional and aesthetic stimuli. It is secondarily concerned with knowledge that builds a background for illumination of experience.

3. Creative attitude in teaching. Music is a vibrant emotional and aesthetic expression very inadequately presented through notation. It is the teacher's responsibility to help children recreate the reality of music so dimly suggested by notation.

4. Acceptance of the "Statement of Beliefs and Purposes" of the Music Educators National Conference, also the following "Creed" written by Osbourne McConathy.

> "Every child should be educated in music according to his natural capacities, at public expense, and his music training should function in the life of the community."

5. An integrated course of study in music. Guard against the tendency to consider many music activities as "extras," to be used spasmodically. For example, preparation for Children's Concerts is for all children as a part of the year's work and attendance upon the concert is desirable but incidental.

6. Psychology of Music Education.
    a. Sensory period—Kindergarten and Grades I, II, and III
       The time for accumulation of all possible musical experience.
    b. Associative period—Grades IV, V, and VI
       The time of drill based upon previous experiences and new musical contacts designed to furnish material for increasing skills and knowledges essential in musical performance.

(*Is this correct? Are you aware of this in your teaching plans?*)

7. Procedure.
   a. Sing, play, listen, and move to gain experience and background
   b. Train accuracy of ear and voice
   c. Develop emotional and aesthetic response to music
   d. Organize experience and develop skills and knowledges through the sense of hearing (Ear Training)
   e. Develop skills and knowledges through sense of sight (Eye Training)
   f. Extension of topic "e" into the field of new material (Music Reading)
   g. Constant expansion of experience through musical performance of rote and reading songs and also through *active* listening
   h. Provide rich opportunities for the more talented.

8. General intelligence. The higher the I.Q. the better the mastery of skills and knowledges. The borderline groups will never do much reading but can secure deep satisfaction through the performance of good rote songs.

(Do you believe this? Do you evaluate in accordance with known ceilings of accomplishment?)

9. Additional musical activities to be selected on a basis of need, interest, and desirability:
   a. School choirs, small ensembles
   b. Creative activities
   c. Rhythm orchestras, orchestras, bands, small ensembles
   d. Eurythmics, folk dancing, etc.
   e. Piano club, recital club, etc.
   f. Concerts *for* children, concerts *by* children
   g. Musical excursions.

SOURCE MATERIAL

ADMINISTRATIVE PROBLEMS IN MUSIC DEPARTMENTS OF LARGE CITIES
  Music Educators National Conference Yearbook

ALL MUSIC COURSES AS MUSIC APPRECIATION
  Music Educators National Conference

ALTO-TENOR VOICE, THE
  Music Educators Journal

AMATEUR IN MUSIC: WHAT, WHY AND HOW, THE
  Staff Meeting of Cleveland Board of Education

ANALYSIS OF TEACHING COSTS BY SUBJECTS
  Music Educators Journal

ANALYZING OBJECTIVES IN MUSIC EDUCATION
  Department of Secondary School Principals, NEA

APPLIED MUSIC CREDITS IN THE SECONDARY SCHOOL FOR PRIVATE STUDY
  Music Teachers National Association

BASIC NEEDS IN AN ELEMENTARY MUSIC EDUCATION PROGRAM
  Staff Bulletin, Cleveland Board of Education

BETTER MUSIC FOR SCHOOL MUSICIANS
  Eastern Division, Music Educators National Conference

BROADCASTING MUSIC TO AMERICAN SCHOOLS
  Music Teachers National Association Yearbook

CAN THE SCHOOLS BE ENTRUSTED WITH THE FUNDAMENTALS OF VOICE BUILDING?
Music Teachers National Association Yearbook

CHALLENGE IN FINE ARTS, THE
Commencement Address, Cleveland Institute of Music

CHALLENGE IN MUSIC EDUCATION, A
Music Educators National Conference Yearbook

CHALLENGE TO MUSIC AS A PROFESSION, A
Sinfonian

CHANGES IN CLASSROOM TEACHING
Staff Meeting of Cleveland Board of Education

CHANGING PHILOSOPHY IN MUSIC EDUCATION, A
Central Ohio Teachers Association

CHARACTERISTICS OF AN EFFECTIVE CITIZEN
University of Hawaii

CHORIC SPEECH AND CHORAL TRAINING
Educational Music Magazine

CLASS INSTRUMENTAL LESSONS IN SCHOOL TIME
Music Educators National Conference Yearbook

CONCERT MUSIC TO WIDEN EXPERIENCES
Department of Elementary School Principals, *Yearbook*, Chapter IV

CONTRIBUTIONS TO RELIGIOUS LIFE OF THE COMMUNITY BY SCHOOL MUSIC TEACHERS
Supervisors Service Bulletin

CREATIVE ATTITUDE IN SECONDARY SCHOOL MUSIC
Junior and Senior High School Clearing House

CREATIVE EXPERIENCE IN MUSIC EDUCATION, THE
Education; Eastern Division of Music Educators National Conference

CURRICULUM AS A MUSICAL EXPERIENCE, THE
North Central Division of Music Educators National Conference

DANGERS IN OVER-PROMOTING MUSIC EDUCATION ACTIVITIES
  Triad, Ohio Music Educators Association
DEVELOPING A PROGRAM FOR MUSIC EDUCATION
  Music Educators National Conference Yearbook
DOES MUSIC EDUCATION PAY?
  East Cleveland Kiwanis Club
EAR TRAINING
  National Society for the Study of Education, *35th Yearbook*
EDUCATION THROUGH SCHOOL MUSIC
  Staff Meeting of Cleveland Board of Education
EDUCATIONAL GUIDANCE IN MUSIC
  Ohio Music Educators Association
EFFECTIVE PROCEDURES IN DEVELOPING MUSICIANSHIP
  In-and-About Boston Music Educators Association
FEASIBLE CREDIT COURSES IN HIGH SCHOOL MUSIC
  Second Educational Symposium, MENC
FINDING AN EDUCATIONAL BASIS FOR THE SCHOOL ORCHESTRA
  Orchestra Section, MENC
GOING ON THE AIR
  Audio-Visual Section, MENC
GRADUATE STUDY IN THE FIELD OF MUSIC EDUCATION
  Music Teachers National Association Yearbook
GUIDANCE SPECIALIST IN MUSIC, THE
  North Central Division of Music Educators National
  Conference
H. S. MUSICIAN INSPECTS THE MUSIC IN HIS COMMUNITY, THE
  Musical Educators National Conference
HIGHER VALUES IN MUSIC EDUCATION, THE
  Staff Meeting of Cleveland Board of Education
HOW THE SCHOOL BRINGS MUSIC INTO THE HOME
  Radio Broadcast, WTAM Cleveland
HOW TO LISTEN TO MUSIC
  Staff Meeting of Cleveland Board of Education

INSTRUMENTAL MUSIC TRAINING OR EDUCATION
  Colorado State Teachers College
INTELLECTUAL FACTORS IN MUSIC APPRECIATION
  Staff Meeting of Cleveland Board of Education
LISTENING TO MUSIC
  Radio Broadcast, American Youth Series, NBC-WTAM, Cleveland
MECHANISTIC APTITUDE AND INTERPRETATIVE POWER IN MUSIC
  Ohio State Educational Conference
MODERN TRENDS IN SCHOOL MUSIC
  Eastern Division of Music Educators National Conference
MUSIC AND A NEW WORLD
  Educational Music Magazine
MUSIC AND THE TAXPAYER
  Rotary Club, Los Angeles, California
MUSIC AS EDUCATION
  Education; Eastern Division of MENC
MUSIC AS AN EDUCATIVE FACTOR
  Cape Girardeau, Missouri
MUSIC AS AN INTEGRATED PROGRAM
  Staff Meeting of Cleveland Board of Education
MUSIC CURRICULUM IN PUBLIC SCHOOLS, THE
  A Report to the Music Teachers National Association
MUSIC EDUCATION AND DEMOCRACY
  Ohio Music Educators Association
MUSIC EDUCATION AND PRESENT DAY PROBLEMS
  Northern Kentucky Education Association
MUSIC EDUCATION IN THE CLEVELAND SCHOOLS
  Report to the Superintendent, Cleveland Board of Education
MUSIC EDUCATION IN POST-WAR PLANNING
  Music Teachers National Association
MUSIC IN SCHOOL INSTRUCTION
  Review of Educational Research

Music in the Junior High School
  Staff Meeting of Cleveland Board of Education
Music Makers in the United States
  Radio Broadcast, WHK Cleveland
Musicianship Requirements for the Music Educator
  Eastern Division of Music Educators National Conference
New Social Attitude in Music Instruction, A
  Columbia University
Our Program of Music Education
  Report to The Superintendent, Cleveland Board of Education
Permanent Values from Music Study
  Commencement Address, John Adams High School,
  Cleveland
Philosophy and Practice in Music Education
  Southeastern Tennessee Teachers Association
Power of Music, The
  Los Angeles *Times*
Preparation for Music Educators
  Ohio State Teachers Association
Present and Future Trends in Public Education Affecting
Music in the Junior High Schools
  Music Educators National Conference Yearbook
Present Trends in Music Education
  Western Reserve University
Program of Music Education, A
  North Central Association Quarterly
Public School Music and the Church Choir
  Sinfonian
Public Schools and Music Listening, The
  Music Teachers National Association
Public Schools and Their Relationship to the Private
Music Teacher
  Ohio Music Teachers Association